twitter
Power

twitter
Power

How to Dominate Your Market
One Tweet at a Time

JOEL COMM

WILEY

John Wiley & Sons, Inc.

For Mary, my wife of more than 20 years. My love for you grows every day. And for my kids, Z and J. You are both awesome and I can't wait to see the great things God has in store for you!

Ten percent of author proceeds for this book go to WaterIsLife.com, a nonprofit organization working to provide clean drinking water to a portion of the one-half billion of the world's population who are deprived of our most basic need. I encourage you to join me in supporting this truly worthwhile cause at www.WaterIsLife.com.

Contents

FOREWORD

Every day 60 million e-mails are sent out around the world. My-Space alone has over 186 million users! Technology has given us so many ways of communicating, but are we truly connecting or just corresponding? Are we adding people into our lives who share our values or merely collecting a list of profiles? Are we deepening relationships or just maintaining them?

As much as we want to nurture every relationship, advances in technology have given us access to more relationships and less time to deepen them. And yet what most of us know, and what I have discovered working with more than 3.5 million people from over 80 countries, is that the quality of our lives is the quality of our relationships. And since life is relationships, relationships follow the rules of life—they either grow or die. Your relationships are as strong or deep as you choose to make them. If you spend quality time in your intimate relationships, if you connect with your families and your friends, those relationships will flourish. If you nurture your relationships with your clients and really meet their needs at a higher level, you build long-lasting connections. Conversely, if you don't grow your customers, you go out of business. If you don't reach your family or friends, those relationships get stripped of the substance and texture they deserve.

Ken Blanchard once described life as a game of Monopoly—no matter how many properties we buy or how many houses we build, at the end of the game "it all goes back in the box." All we have ultimately are the relationships that we nurtured, the lives that we impacted, and the ones that have touched us. All we have are the experiences that we have shared. When two people meet, a third world is created. And with today's technology, that world can grow exponentially.

Technology such as Twitter has the potential to give us more than just an opportunity to tell others what happened in our day. If we understand and appreciate what Twitter is capable of, we can use it to instantly share our lives with others, and we can use it to reach more people in a meaningful way. Imagine if you could share the magic moments in the days of your kids or family that otherwise you would have missed. Imagine if you had cost-efficient and fast marketing tools that met existing customers where they are and that also helped you acquire new customers. Imagine if you had the power to build a network of like-minded peers, a community of shared ideas and creativity.

In *Twitter Power*, Joel Comm provides us with the tools, techniques, and benefits for growing our network of resources to create even more fulfilling connections. He shows us the powerful uses of Twitter for brand expansion, building a community that ultimately enriches us personally and professionally and allows us to grow and contribute beyond ourselves.

Joel explains the effortless ways we can make a contribution by being a mentor as well as sharing in the interests and passions of others. In *Twitter Power*, Joel teaches us how we can use technology not just to correspond, but also to connect. He shows us how the Internet can give us the freedom to experience the depth of relationships, and how it can help us achieve and sustain an extraordinary quality of life—a life of meaning.

With deep respect,

Anthony Robbins
Peak performance coach
Chairman, Robbins Research International, Inc.
Author of *Unlimited Power* and *Awaken the Giant Within*

The Power of Twitter

November 26, 2008—Mumbai Rocked by Shootings

The first news headlines and photos of the devastating terror attack in India shocked the world as more than 300 people lost their lives and countless more were injured.

Once again, we banded together as civilized people and poured out our compassion and aid for those affected by this senseless tragedy.

But what was equally amazing was the medium in which those first headlines and photos were delivered.

It wasn't CNN.

It wasn't National Public Radio.

And it wasn't *The New York Times*.

No, the first accounts of what was taking place in Mumbai, and the headline stated above, were written by regular people who were on the scene. They wisely used a Web site called Twitter to broadcast breaking news.

Just minutes after the initial attack, the following messages were broadcast on Twitter's site:

Urvaksh: "mumbai is in chaos. 18 dead, 40 held hostage at Oberoi, a five star hotel, firing going on at a JW Marriott." 11:33 AM Nov 26, from the Web

Fossiloflife: "gun battles happening at two strategic points of south Mumbai" 10:34 AM Nov 26, from the Web

It was hours later before the first reports of the terror attack appeared on broadcast news.

CNN eventually ran a story titled, "Tweeting the Terror: How Social Media Responded to Mumbai."

While I gave careful, thoughtful consideration to beginning a business book using this terrible tragedy as an example, nothing better demonstrates how technology has changed the way we communicate and interact.

We now live in a time where ordinary citizens are empowered to be conduits of information to the masses like never before. The major media outlets can not report as quickly or accurately as those who are actually on the scene.

And whether we are talking about breaking news or opportunities to harness this same technology to grow your business, it's clear that the future belongs to those who embrace social media as regular part of their lives.

Just as breaking news is now more breaking than ever, businesses can harness the immediacy of Twitter to innovate and build relationships like never before.

That's powerful.

It's Twitter Power.

What Can Twitter Do for You?

Online marketing is a fantastic way to build a business. You can do it from your own home, at your own pace, according to your own schedule and sometimes even without startup costs.

Providing advice and promoting products across the Web has helped me to build a successful seven-figure company. It started in my bedroom and has since taken me on speaking tours across the country and around the world.

But creating an Internet business—even a small one—does require work, and part of that work involves staying up to date with the newest tools and the latest online innovations.

That's not as easy as it sounds. Not every "next big thing" turns out be a giant. The Web is littered with links leading to services that promised a great deal, delivered little, and faded away. Part of building a successful online business means knowing which tools are likely to be useful revenue-generators and which are going to be major time-wasters.

Sometimes, that's obvious. It was pretty clear when Facebook and MySpace came along that they were going to be both powerful and useful. The ability to renew old friendships and maintain current ones with very little effort—and for no cost—was always going to attract large numbers of people. And the ease with which entrepreneurs could use those sites to build networks and keep their market interested and engaged meant that an understanding of social media has become hugely important for online marketers.

The value of Twitter was far less obvious.

The system really couldn't be any simpler. It lets anyone send a message no longer than 140 characters that answers the question "What are you doing now?"

You can send that message at any time, from your computer or from your mobile phone, and it can be seen by anyone who has chosen to follow those messages.

That's really all there is to it.

I told you it was simple.

It doesn't sound like much, and for Internet entrepreneurs used to writing 300- to 500-word blog posts several times a week, it also sounds painfully restrictive.

What on Earth can you put in 140 characters that could possibly be worth reading?

Surely you can't promote products, build a brand, generate interest in your company, and keep people reading with such small amounts of content?

The answers, it turns out, are "a lot" and "yes, you really can!"

Twitter has proven itself to be incredibly addictive and, for business owners, very valuable too.

Ever since I stumbled onto Twitter, I've spent many hours thumb-typing messages. I do it frequently and I love it. It's fantastic fun, like writing a personal blog but without the effort.

The pleasure alone would be enough reason for me to recommend Twitter, but Twitter isn't just good fun. It's also proven to be a very important and easy way of finding new users and customers, a powerful networking tool, and an excellent way of picking up useful information.

It's helped me to build deeper relationships with my partners, my clients, and other entrepreneurs.

It's extended the reach of my brand, making the name of my business known to people who might never otherwise have heard of it.

It's brought me advice and suggestions from experts I couldn't have reached any other way.

It brings me a steady stream of additional Web site users and provides a channel for me to alert people who have visited my sites when I've uploaded new content.

And it's brought me some fascinating reading and a bunch of wonderful new friends, too.

In this book, I'm going to explain what you can do to get the most out of Twitter and make microblogging—the sending of tiny messages—work for your business.

I'll start with a quick introduction to social media. Twitter grew out of the online networking craze that had given sites like MySpace and Facebook such giant valuations. Although Twitter can work wonders when used alone, it's at its most powerful when combined with other social media tools. This book will focus on Twitter, but I'll begin with an overview of social media sites so that you'll find it easy to connect your microblogging with other forms of online networking.

I'll then describe Twitter. I'll explain how it works, what the service can do, and exactly why it's so powerful. The site might look small, but it packs a surprising punch. I'll explain the reason behind Twitter's super powers.

Then I'll start to get practical. I'll talk you through signing up to Twitter and selecting a username. Both of those are fairly straight-forward (even if it is easy to make expensive mistakes), but Twitter also lets its members create profiles to introduce themselves to other users. The profiles are pretty basic. You won't find any of the fancy bells and whistles that you can expect to see on other social networking sites. But that doesn't mean you should stick to the fundamentals.

Your profile is an important marketing page. With a little thought and just a touch of creativity, it can function as a useful entry point to your commercial site and help raise the profile of your business. I'll discuss what to include, how to design it, and how to make the page pay.

I'll then talk about the most important thing you'll need to know on Twitter: how to build a following.

That's vital. Although every message—or "tweet," as they're called on Twitter—is public, if no one knows you're there, no one will know to read them.

There's a huge list of different strategies that Twitterers are using to build up followers, make new contacts, and keep in touch. Some of them are very simple. Others are a little more complex and require a bit of thought—and sometimes even a little expense, too.

I'll talk you through some of the most effective ways that I've discovered to build up followers.

Finding followers isn't difficult. Much harder is keeping them. That's only going to happen if you create the sort of content that people actually want to read.

There's nothing new about that. Anyone who has ever tried to generate revenue with a Web site knows that content is king. When you can write articles and posts of any length you want, upload videos, and show off your images, there are plenty of options and lots of flexibility. When you're restricted to a message of no more than 140 characters, though, creating interesting content sounds much more challenging.

It *is* more challenging, but it's also a lot more fun. You can do it quickly, without making great demands on your audience and—once you get used to it—without a great deal of thought.

I'll explain what makes good Twitter content and talk you through some of the sorts of messages that successful Twitterers are sending.

Tweets, though, are just a means to an end. The goal of using Twitter is to build relationships—especially relationships that can benefit your company. In the following two chapters, I look at how connecting with two different types of followers can bring those benefits.

I discuss connecting with customers on Twitter by problem-solving, winning referrals, and supplying support; and I talk about using Twitter to communicate with team members, especially when they're scattered in different places.

Once you've built up your following and are enjoying using Twitter, you can start to make all that effort pay off. There are a number of ways to do that, and I'll talk about them in detail as well.

The first is brand extension. Twitter can be a very effective branding tool for any business, and it's been used by some of the world's largest companies to drum up publicity for their products. I'll discuss ways you can use your tweets and your followers to extend the power of your company's name, as well as the rules for effective brand-building with Twitter.

Blog posts can also be promoted using Twitter—an important way to turn your followers not just into visitors but also into cash—and so can stores and other retail outlets. Although Twitter is not strictly a commercial area, with carefully written content, it is possible to directly increase your conversions and make extra sales.

And like Facebook, Twitter has also created a network of add-ons and applications that help its users get even more out of the service. I'll introduce you to some of the most useful and, in Chapter 11, explain how to add powerful solutions to the Twitter platform.

Finally, I'll provide a 30-day step-by-step plan for dominating Twitter that will take you from a Twitter Johnny-No-Friends to a powerful social networking force in just one month.

Twitter is very restrictive. It doesn't allow users to make videos, upload rich media content, or do any of the fancy things you might have become accustomed to on other sites.

Nor is it a sales arena. Although businesses are using Twitter to increase their revenues and make money, thinking of the site as a low-cost—even free—way to advertise is not going to bring results.

In fact, that's just going to cost you time you could have spent doing something far more rewarding.

At its most basic, Twitter is a communication tool. It's a channel that lets you speak to lots of people and enlighten them about your life and your work.

You can think of it as a giant virtual water cooler. It's a place where people come to get to know each other, to make friends, to network, and, most importantly, to converse.

It's not a place where people come to sell—and pushing sales hard on Twitter just isn't going to work.

On the other hand, if you do manage to build up friends on Twitter, you should find that those friends see you as the first stop for the products or services they need.

People always prefer to do business with people they know, and they get to know them by talking to them and swapping ideas with them.

On the Internet, people are doing that on Twitter.

While I will provide you with various examples, I will use my own experiences with Twitter as an ongoing case study throughout this book. After all, Twitter is about relationships. It only makes sense to provide you with an up-close look at how I have used the site to build relationships and grow my business.

twitter
Power

An Introduction to the Social Media Landscape

Once upon a time, anyone could be a media publisher. All you needed was several million dollars, a team of editors and writers, a printing press capable of shooting out a dozen copies a second, and a distribution network that would put your publication in stores across the country.

Unless, of course, you wanted to go into radio or television. In that case, things were just a little harder.

The result was that information came down. We didn't talk among ourselves; we were talked to by writers, editors, and producers, who chose the subjects and told us what they thought. If we liked what we were reading, we kept tuning in and the company made money. If we didn't like it, we stopped buying the magazine or we switched channels. When that happened, advertisers turned away, and all of the millions of dollars required to create the publication disappeared.

Today, it's all so very different. It can cost literally nothing to create content and make it available for other people to enjoy. That low cost means that it doesn't matter if it's not read by millions. You can focus on a small market—even one interested in stamp collecting in Mozambique—and still find enough people to form a community and maybe even make a profit through advertising and product sales.

It's called the "long tail," and the Internet has made fantastic use of it.

But the low cost of publishing online has had another effect: We aren't being talked to by professional writers and publishers any more; we're talking to each other.

Average folk like you and me—the kind of people who didn't study journalism at university, who never spent years as a cub reporter covering local court cases, and who were never even very good at Scrabble, let alone putting together articles—are writing about the topics they love and sharing their views.

And they're hearing back too. The conversation is flowing in both directions.

Anyone now can launch a Web site, write articles, or even create videos and put them live. And anyone can comment on that content, affecting both its nature and the direction of the publication.

That's social media, and it's a publishing revolution.

So What Exactly Is Social Media?

Social media can be all sorts of different things, and it can be produced in all sorts of different ways. Perhaps the best definition of social media, though, is content that has been created by its audience.

Facebook, for example, is not a publishing company. It doesn't create any of its own content. It doesn't write articles or posts, and it doesn't upload films or images for people to view and enjoy.

It allows its users to do all of that on its behalf.

It's as though Fox were to fire all its actors, producers, news anchors, and scriptwriters, throw open its doors, and tell the world that anyone is welcome to come in and shoot their own programs.

And then let them broadcast those programs on its networks for nothing too.

Of course, if that were to happen, you'd still have to tell people what channel you were on and when they could see your program. You'd still have to produce content that other people might actually enjoy. And inevitably, the people who took the most professional approach, put time and effort into what they were doing, and connected with their audiences would be the most successful.

But even that wouldn't allow viewers to take part in the program, something which forms an important part of social media.

Create a group on a site like Facebook and you won't be expected to supply all of the text and all of the images. You'll be expecting other group members to add their stories and photographs too.

Even bloggers, when they write a post, expect their readers to join the discussion by leaving comments at the bottom of the post that take the argument in new directions and add new information.

This is the "social" part of social media, and it means that publishing is now about participation.

Someone who uses social media successfully doesn't just create content; he or she creates conversations.

And those conversations create communities.

That's the real beauty of social media, and while it may or may not be the goal—depending on the site—the result of social media can always be firm connections between the people who participate.

When those connections are formed around businesses, the results can be the sort of brand loyalty and commitment that sales professionals have been dreaming about since the first days of direct marketing.

The definition of social media then is a vague thing. At its broadest, it describes a form of publishing in which stories are swapped rather than published and the exchange of content happens within a community, rather like a chat in a restaurant.

At its narrowest, it describes one way in which publishers and marketers can put their messages in front of thousands of people and encourage them to build strong connections and firm loyalty.

However it's defined though, social media has proved incredibly popular.

Facebook claims to have over 60 million active members—that's *active* members, not just people who created a profile and never used it. It's averaged 250,000 new registrations every day since the beginning of 2007, doubling the number of active users every six months. More than half of those users return every day and together they generate more than 65 *billion* pages views each month.

According to their own statistics, MySpace, which went live shortly before Facebook, is even more popular, with more than 110 million people using the site at least once a month. One in four

Americans is said to be on MySpace, and in the United Kingdom, as many people own a MySpace account as own a dog.

The site has generated around 14 billion user comments and 10 billion friend relationships and sees more than 8 million images uploaded each day.

Twitter, which was launched more than two years after MySpace—a lifetime in Internet terms—isn't quite in the same numeric league, but it's growth has still been phenomenal. As a company that currently relies on venture capital, it can be pretty cagy about its membership figures, but in March 2008, it was believed to be sending more than 3 million messages a day between more than a million users, of whom 200,000 were active on a daily basis. Those users have created more than 4 million connections. By October 2008, TwitDir (www.twitdir.com), a directory of Twitter users, was reporting that it knew of 3,262,795 Twitterers.

There is another fact about Twitter that's particularly interesting, though . . .

It's massively underused.

According to the site's own blog, around half of all Twitterers follow and are followed by just 10 people. The top 10 percent of Twitterers have more than 80 followers and follow more than 70 people.

To join the top 10 percent of Twitter users, then, you just need to attract 80 followers!

To put that into perspective, as of this writing I have almost 5,000 followers and follow around 1,700 people! (I get about 25 new followers each day.) It's not difficult to do, and when you know how, it shouldn't take you much time at all.

All of these figures just scratch the surface of the popularity of social media. YouTube attracts more than 60 million unique visitors each month. They tune into the 10 hours of video footage uploaded to the site every minute.

Throw in the countless numbers of blogs (Technorati tracks more than 100 million English language blogs alone), and it becomes pretty clear that social media is a massive phenomenon that's changing the way all of us create and use content—and the way that businesses use that content and their distribution channels, too.

Social Media, So What? Why Social Media Really Is a Big Deal

So we can see that social media sites can be big. Really, really big. But so what? There are lots of people in the telephone book, and that's very big too. It doesn't make it a particularly useful marketing tool.

Social media sites don't just list people, though, and they don't just list any old people.

Each site lists a very special group of people.

At first glance, that might seem a little strange. Whether you're browsing through Facebook, MySpace, Flickr, or Twitter, you're going to see small pictures of people, small messages to and from people, and profiles in which those people say certain things about themselves, such as where they work, where they're from, and what they do in their spare time.

Look a little closer, though, and you'll start to notice a few differences. Although the sites may seem very similar, in fact, each site has its own unique feel and its own unique demographic.

Because Facebook started at Harvard, for example (it had signed up half the undergraduate population within a month of going live), and because initially it was restricted to university students, it has a high percentage of well-educated members. The site boasts that it has an 85 percent market share of four-year universities and that "more than half of Facebook users are outside of college."

Clearly, that suggests many of Facebook's users are still in college—a fantastic market for companies hoping to pick up customers, start those customers in the habit of buying from them, and stay with them as their income rises.

Facebook isn't unique in having highly educated members. Twitter's membership might currently be smaller than that of many other social media sites, but it appears to be very selective—even if it is self-selective.

Tracking Twitter's demographics isn't easy. Although some people have had fun following the frequency with which certain wealth-related terms (such as well-to-do neighborhoods) turn up (they found themselves following lots of local lawyers as a result), there's no way to easily conduct a demographic survey of the site's users.

However, Hitwise, an Internet monitoring service, did manage to produce some very interesting and some very impressive results.

Writing in *Time* magazine in August 2008, Bill Tancer, Hitwise's general manager of research and author of *Click: What Millions Do Online and Why It Matters*, noted that he had discovered that Twitter is 63 percent male and, at that time, 57 percent of its U.S. visitors (although not necessarily its members) were Californian—a statistic that likely reflects the site's large attraction to high-tech workers. Twitter itself points out that 60 percent of its Web traffic comes from outside the United States, though—in particular, Japan, Spain, and the United Kingdom. It also notes that had it looked at other ways of accessing the site, such as SMS, the international breakdown would have been very different.

More interestingly, according to Bill Tancer, Twitter's largest age demographic is now 35- to 44-year-olds. They make up just over a quarter of its users, a shift from its starting point among 18- to 24-year-olds.

Most fascinating of all, though, Tancer also says that just over 14 percent of Twitter's visitors are what he calls "Stable Career" types—a "collection of young and ethnically diverse singles living in big-city metros like Los Angeles, Philadelphia, and Miami." Another 12 percent are "Young Cosmopolitans"—40-somethings *with household incomes of over $250,000 per year*.

That means that Twitter isn't just used by young people as an alternative to SMS. The site has a large following among older, professional audiences, too, and a full quarter of Twitter's users are high-earners, a valuable piece of information that makes the site a must-use for any serious marketer.

So we can see that social media sites aren't just attracting kids looking for places to chat with their friends and find free music downloads. They're also attracting smart, educated people with money to burn.

And they're attracting experts, too.

You can see this most clearly on specialist sites like Flickr, a photo-sharing service. Although Flickr, too, isn't very forthcoming about its demographic details, spend any time at all on the site and you can't help but notice the number of professional photographers who use it.

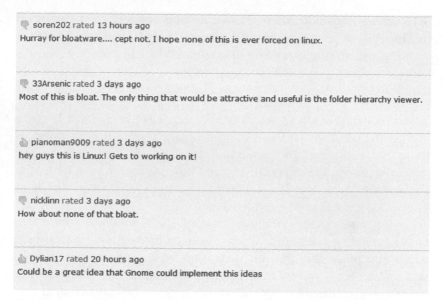

Figure 1.1   Know what these StumbleUpon users are talking about? Me neither . . .

Part of the site's appeal isn't just the pictures; it's the advice enthusiasts can pick up from experts working in their field and ready to share the benefits of their experience.

Even a social bookmarking site like StumbleUpon can generate some very expert comments in the reviews of the sites submitted by users.

So we can see that social media sites attract absolutely huge numbers of people. We can see, too, that many of those people are highly educated, are paid well, and are experts in their fields.

You should be able to see very clearly then that social media offers a gigantic opportunity for any business owner to promote his or her products to exactly the sort of market he or she want to reach.

The Different Types of Social Media Sites— Content to Suit Every Market

One of the reasons that social media has proved to be so popular is that it's available in all sorts of different forms. While the networking sites with their tens of millions of members might be the most familiar, there are actually all sorts of different ways of creating and sharing social media content:

BLOGS

Yes, blogs are a form of social media too. They're written by people on every topic you can imagine. And only a tiny fraction of them are produced by professionals, even though all have the potential to generate revenue. Even my mother has a blog that she uses to describe her travel experiences. (You can see it at TravelsWithSheila.com—tell her I said "hi.")

What really makes blogging part of social media is that it can cost nothing to use. Sure, if you want to have your own domain name and place the blog on your own server, you might have to pay a small fee—and when I say "small," I mean less than $20 per month. And there are strategies you can use to bring in readers that will cost money too.

But you don't actually need to do any of that.

Figure 1.2   My blog's home page. I write it, you read it ... and comment on it.

To become a blogger, you don't need to do any more than sign up at Blogger.com or WordPress.com any of the other free blogging services and start writing.

Within minutes, you'll be creating content and you'll form a part of the social media world.

However, blogs do take some effort. They have to be updated regularly, and while you can put anything on a blog, from short posts to feature-length videos if you want, you'll have to work to keep your readers entertained, informed, and engaged. It's fun stuff, and it can be very profitable stuff too but it's not a sweat-free business.

Most importantly, while you can accept guest posts and hire writers, and although your comments will be a crucial element of your site's attraction, it will still be *you* guiding the content and setting the subjects.

Blogs *are* a form of social media, but it's a society with a clear ruler.

MEMBERSHIP SITES

That top-down feel that can be present in some social media channels is also present in membership sites. There are far fewer of these on the Web than there are blogs, but there's still no shortage of them, and like any social media site, they rely on the members to produce the content that's the site's attraction.

My own membership site, for example, is TopOneNetwork.com. With just under 1,000 members, it's a long way behind Facebook, but it's not intended to be a site for the masses. It's meant to be selective and targeted only toward people who are really determined to succeed at online marketing.

I use the site for coaching and to share valuable marketing information with other top marketers, but the heart of the site is the activity that takes place between its members.

I might like to believe that it's my advice and lessons that keep everyone coming back, but a quick look at what people are discussing in the groups shows that there's a lot more to it than that. My members have been swapping fantastic ideas and creating the sorts of connections that lead to valuable deals and joint ventures.

That wouldn't happen if the site was much more general. If TopOneNetwork.com wasn't carefully targeted, it would be too

Figure 1.3 My membership site at TopOneNetwork.com functions in much the same way as a social media site. Just check out the number of friendships and comments my members generate.

difficult for marketers to find each other, network, and share the information that keeps them on the site.

But that doesn't mean membership sites can't be massive. Dating sites like Match.com are a form of social media, too. The content that people are paying to use consists of the profiles and pictures that the site's members have created and uploaded.

Match might have an online magazine, but no one is paying $25 every month to read the magazine. They're paying that price month after month to read the descriptions and look at the photos that other people have posted, and to contact those people.

It's not the site that's the attraction of social media sites; it's the society.

SQUIDOO

Squidoo doesn't look like a social media site. You don't get to make connections or build giant piles of friends in the same way that you can on other social media sites. But what you can do is create your

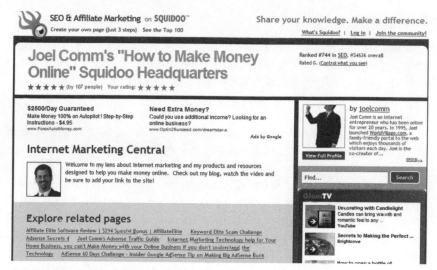

Figure 1.4   My lens on Squidoo. All my own work.

own content and act as a hub through which people looking for the information you're supplying can pass.

The site is intended to be the first stop for anyone looking for information on any topic. It's a place where experts can provide basic information and tell people where they need to go to learn more.

I've been on Squidoo for some time now, and I've found it to be a lot of fun and pretty rewarding, too. The site provides you with a free Web page—it calls them "lenses"—which you can construct using their modules, so it's very easy to use. All you have to do is place your own content in those modules. You even get a share of the advertising revenue, depending on the popularity of your lens.

And that's where the social aspect comes in again. Yes, Squidoo depends on its members to produce the content that users want, but it also depends on the community to identify which lenses are worth viewing. That makes networking vital.

While you can't add someone as a contact on Squidoo, as you promote your lens, you will inevitably end up making plenty of new friends.

PHOTO SITES

Squidoo relies mostly on links as the most important form of content on its lenses. Lensmasters are intended to help users find the knowledge they need somewhere else, rather than supply all of that information themselves. Squidoo only provides one page, after all.

But links certainly aren't the only form of content that can be shared or that require active networks to make sure that they're seen.

Ever since cameras went digital, there's been a need for a low-cost—or even free—way to share those images with anyone who wants to see them online. Both Facebook and MySpace allow their users to upload their images, but neither of them is a dedicated photography site. Images are just one form of content that users are free to share on those sites, together with videos, personal histories, group discussions, etc.

There are sites, however, that specialize in photography. They depend entirely on the photos that users upload to bring in other users.

That broad-based content sourcing already makes sites like Flickr—one of the most popular photo-sharing sites, and now

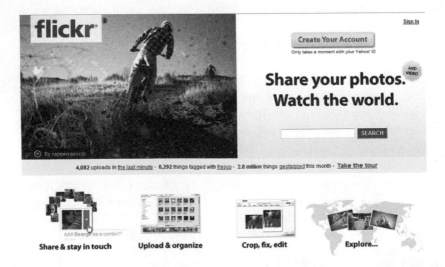

Figure 1.5   Flickr is the big daddy of photo-sharing Web sites.

owned by Yahoo!—part of the social media phenomenon, but Flickr also has the networking power of those sites.

Like Facebook and MySpace, it's possible to create long lists of friends, and you can join groups where you can submit images, enter competitions, and join discussions about the best way to light a child's portrait or which lens to use in which conditions.

Flickr also allows its members to mark images as favorites and to place comments beneath them. Both of those activities can be valuable ways of adding new friends. Pro members, who pay a subscription fee of $24.95 per year, can even see stats that indicate how many views, faves, and comments each image has produced, and even where their visitors came from.

All of that networking is vital to success on the site, and that success can have some spectacular results. In 2006, Rebekka Gudsleifdottir, an Icelandic art student whose images and networking had brought her a huge following on Flickr, was spotted by an advertising executive on the site who hired her to shoot a series of billboard ads for the Toyota Prius. Many of the images used in Windows Vista, too, were bought from photographers commissioned after they were discovered on the site.

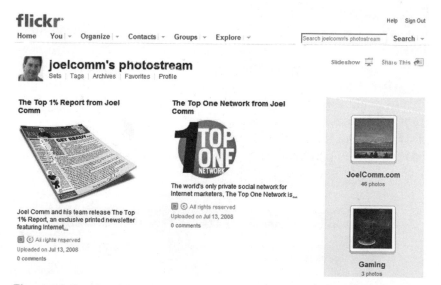

Figure 1.6   Yes, I have a Flickr stream too. You can even see my house on it.

Every day, images are licensed and prints are sold on Flickr, and it's all based on content created by the site's users and promoted through careful networking.

That's classic social media.

MICROBLOGS

And finally, we come to microblogging. This is a whole new thing in social media. In some ways, it's the exact opposite of everything we've seen so far.

Social media sites tend to want their members to contribute as much content as possible. They may restrict that content to just photographs (or, on Flickr, video now as well), or they may restrict membership to a select few (in the case of my membership site, to dedicated Internet marketers; in the case of dating sites, to dedicated singles), but on the whole, they want their members to offer as much content as possible.

Microblog sites place strict limits on the content that can be uploaded . . . and they find that those limits encourage creativity.

A Closer Look at Microblogging

Just as there are many different kinds of social media sites, so there are many different ways to microblog. One of the most popular now actually takes place within the larger, general social media sites.

When Facebook realized that many of its members loved the idea of being able to update their contacts in real time, they added their own microblogging system.

Facebook's system only works within the site, though, so unlike Twitter, which can broadcast your tweets to mobile telephones as

Figure 1.7 Facebook catches up with microblogging.

well, updates are only visible to friends who happen to be on the site at the time.

For Facebook users, though, it's still very powerful—and Twitter users who want their updates to reach further can use Facebook's Twitter application. This lets them send tweets from within Facebook itself. I use it and I think it's great. You can find it at www.facebook.com/apps/application.php?id=2231777543, or by searching the apps for Twitter.

Facebook isn't the only social media site to try to add microblogging to its list of features. LinkedIn, a social networking site geared towards professional connections, has integrated a system that lets people share information about what they're working on.

Just as importantly, the site also lets its users track what people are saying in those posts with a very neat application called "Company Buzz."

This is the first time that microblogging has been geared specifically to a business audience, and it's easy to understand the value this could have for a firm that wants to understand what its employees, customers, and suppliers are saying about it.

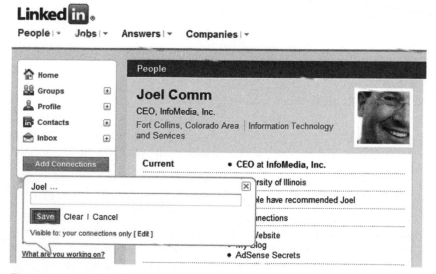

Figure 1.8   Microblogging the LinkedIn way.

Figure 1.9   Spoink is microblogging in rich media.

SPOINK

Pownce does what Twitter does and expands it by removing the restrictions and increasing the type of content that can be sent. Spoink (www.spoink.com) takes the trend even further, allowing its users to do things as complicated as posting audio content through a telephone. It also allows instant messaging across a range of different platforms, and e-mail too.

For a microblogging service, it's complicated. That certainly doesn't mean it's useless; it has a lot of different uses. But unless you have a particular challenge you need to overcome in rich media, I think it's likely to be most effective as a communication tool to join together different platforms than a main way of keeping lots of people informed.

YAMMER

Microblog services thrive most when they ask users to answer a simple question and allow anyone to see the answer. Yammer (www.yammer.com) keeps to those microblogging roots, but narrows the focus of the question—and the audience, too.

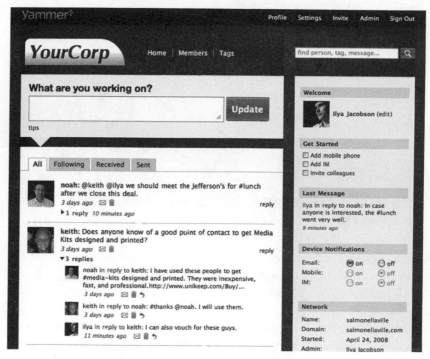

Figure 1.10 Yammer's restrictions make Twitter look like a free-for-all.

Instead of inviting people to share what they're doing (and receiving answers that might range from saving an oil-soaked bird to eating an avocado sandwich), it asks users to explain what they're working on, like LinkedIn. But it only reveals those answers to people on the network with the same corporate e-mail address.

That makes it a useful tool for communicating within a business, but it's not so handy for mass marketing.

PLURK

Plurk (www.plurk.com) might have a terrible name, but it does have some excellent ideas. You can think of it as MySpace to Twitter's Facebook. Instead of presenting posts (which Plurk naturally calls "plurks") vertically, the site displays them horizontally so that they appear as a timeline.

Figure 1.11   Plurk puts the blog back in microblogging.

In addition to seeing what people said, you get to see when they said it, and in the process, pick up a feel for their day.

Plurks can also come with qualifiers—colored tags such as <shares>, <asks>, or <says>—that mark out the nature of the content, and while they are limited to 140 characters, plurks can include images and videos. You can also restrict them to "cliques," small groups of friends with something in common, like a network.

Less useful is the "Karma" feature, which unlocks features as users are more active on the site. Although it's clearly intended to encourage people to stay active, it can also be a source of frustration for anyone who wants to get the most out of the site right away.

Plurk has only been around since May 2008, and it will be interesting to see how it develops and how many users it picks up. It's likely that while Twitter will continue to attract well-to-do educated types who want to network professionally and mix with other experts, Plurk could become a fun microblogging forum.

Introducing ... Twitter!

And finally, we come to Twitter—the site that has really set the standard in microblogging.

The service was founded by programmers Evan Williams, Jack Dorsey, and Biz Stone in July 2006. Williams was a serial entrepreneur who had founded a company called Pyra Labs that made project management software. A note-taking feature on that software went on to become Blogger, the free blogging service later bought by Google. According to one theory, it was Williams who first used the term "blogger" to describe people who write Web logs.

In 2004, Williams left Google to form podcasting company Odeo and, two years later, created Obvious with Biz Stone, a programmer who had joined Blogger after its acquisition by the search engine giant. The new company bought Odeo, which it later sold to a company called Sonic Mountain. It now focuses on Twitter.

The original idea for Twitter came from Dorsey, an Odeo employee. In an interview for ReadWriteTalk.com with Sean Ammirati, VP of Business Development and Product Management at mSpoke, Stone described the moment when they first discussed the idea:

> *"A few of us were thinking about what are some interesting ways that maybe we can merge SMS to the web," he said. "[Dorsey] had come up with this idea where if you just look at only the status field of an instant message application like AIM, and you just look at that as a sort of really small version of what people are already doing ... and you just make it super simple, 'Here's what I'm doing.' ... [W]e kind of went off in a corner and we worked for two weeks and we created a prototype. We showed the rest of the team and everyone just sort of giggled. They all kind of loved it. It was really fun. We used it over the weekend. We found it very compelling and we decided that we would keep working on it."*

That was in March 2006; initially, Twitter was used by the company's employees as a fun form of internal communication. (Tech companies, it seems, might have lava lamps and space hoppers, but they never seem to have water coolers!)

The service launched officially in October 2006, picked up a South by Southwest Web (SXSW) Award in March 2007, and by April was a separate entity headed by Dorsey.

Figure 1.12   Twitter's iconic "fail whale." Designed by Yiying Lu, the beluga whale supported by twittering birds is now a brand in its own right after its frequent appearance on an overstrained Twitter site.

Helped by the publicity generated by the SXSW award, boosted by references on Blogger (where the company had good connections, of course), and most importantly making itself attractive with an open platform that let other developers extend the service, the site started to take off.

That has led to some problems. In 2007, Twitter was reported to have had just 98 percent uptime—a loss of three whole days over the year—and tended to suffer particularly badly during major tech conferences (which says something about many of its users, too).

It has had some very impressive successes, though. Some of the world's leading personalities, corporations, and government bodies are known to use the service, including Barack Obama (twitter.com/

barackobama), Whole Foods Market (twitter.com/wholefoods) and the British Parliament (twitter.com/UKParliament). The American Red Cross (twitter.com/redcross), too, now uses Twitter as a fast way to communicate information about local disasters.

There are two things that really distinguish Twitter, though.

The first is its simplicity. Although the service now has piles of additional tools and add-ons which extend its use, at its core, Twitter remains nothing more than a way of describing what you're doing in no more than 140 characters.

That brevity and simplicity have always been key, and they're what brought Twitter its second characteristic: critical mass.

The hardest moment for any social Web service is at the beginning. In this chapter, for example, we saw how Plurk offers some promising, fun features, but people are going to be unwilling to join in until they can see who else is there and in particular, whether their friends are on the site.

It takes a special push to get a social media site snowballing to a size big enough for everyone to feel comfortable about climbing on board. For Facebook, that was its marketing at Harvard and from there to other universities.

For Twitter, it was the boost it received with its SXSW Award, which had everyone talking about the service as the next big thing.

As long it has that critical mass—and with more than three million members it certainly has that—Twitter is always going to be the microblogging service to beat. In the next chapter, I'll explain exactly why it's likely to retain that position as the leading microblogging service.

2

What Is Twitter and Why Is It So Powerful?

So Twitter as a whole isn't unique.

Yes, it's big, and that makes it unique among microblogging services (if not among social media sites).

It's got buzz that other sites just don't have.

And it's growing at the kind of phenomenal rate that's already forced the social media giants to look over their shoulders and copy it.

But it's not the only service that allows people to broadcast short messages. We've already seen that there are plenty of other sites that offer the same service in one form or another.

But Twitter is by far the most powerful microblogging service currently available, and marketers absolutely need to be aware of it.

Twitter and Its Successes

I've mentioned that at its simplest, Twitter is just a means to send short updates to people who want to receive them.

The most basic way to do that is to log into your Twitter account on the Web and type your tweet into the text field. Anyone can see all of your outgoing tweets if they choose to look at your profile.

Followers can also see a list of tweets from everyone they follow when they log into their Twitter home pages.

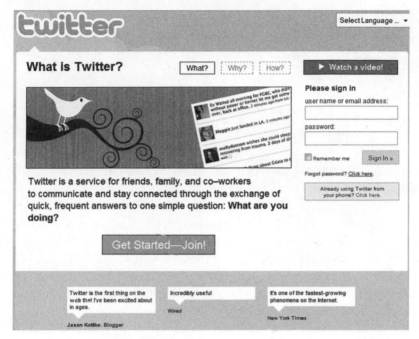

Figure 2.1 Twitter's home page. Your Twitter home page will look a little different.

Your Twitter experience, then, will be made up of sending your own updates and reading tweets from others.

But that's just the start.

One of the inspirations for Twitter was the idea of combining Web-based updates with mobile information. So Twitter makes it possible for mobile phone users to send updates from their handsets, and in some places to receive them on their handsets, too.

So if you had just agreed a joint venture with a marketing partner while sitting in a bar at a conference, and you wanted to share the news right away, you could just pull out your mobile phone and send a quick message to Twitter.

Yes, you might have to pay for that SMS message. You wouldn't pay Twitter. But you would pay your mobile phone company . . . for one message.

Figure 2.2   What my Twitter profile looks like to one of my followers. A message goes out and is visible here ...

Twitter will then pass that message on to all of your followers, including by broadcasting further SMS messages to people who have chosen to receive their updates on their mobiles.

Initially, Twitter footed the bill for that service; later, they negotiated agreements with companies in the United States, Canada, and India. However, users in the United Kingdom—where Twitter failed to broker a deal with communication companies—cannot receive updates by SMS and have to use one of the other mobile services, such as m.twitter.com or TwitterBerry.

For the rest of us though, Twitter can function as a powerful, low-cost SMS broadcasting station.

The benefits that can bring can be huge. I mentioned that the Red Cross have already spotted Twitter's potential and use the site to provide updates related to ongoing disasters.

That's a service that relies on Twitter's speed, numbers, and mobility.

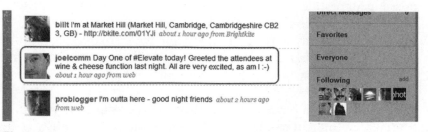

Figure 2.3   ... and arrives at the home page of one of my followers here.

LA Chapter map of active Red Cross shelters http://tinyurl.com/3pymzw
#lafire *9:32 PM Oct 13th from web*

If advised to evacuate, do so immediately. Wear protective clothing, take
important papers, tell someone where you're going. #LAFIRE *3:11 PM Oct 13th
from web*

CA Wildfire evacuation shelter is at San Fernando High School San
Fernando High School 11133 Omelveny Ave San Fernando, CA 91340
#LAFIRE *2:55 PM Oct 13th from web*

Red Cross shelter and map of evac. area available at LAFD blog
http://tinyurl.com/4wqo69 *2:42 PM Oct 13th from web*

@bbarreda You can register yourself as safe & well online
https://disastersafe.redcro... *2:41 PM Oct 13th from web in reply to bbarreda*

@stangel safety guide for when wldfre threatens - if you have time
http://tinyurl.com/4jc3fg #LAFIRE *2:35 PM Oct 13th from web in reply to stangel*

CA Wildfires started yesterday about 20 miles north of LA, burning 750
acres. Santa Ana winds could feed the fire. One shelter already open. *12:20
PM Oct 13th from web*

**Figure 2.4 The American Red Cross's tweets (twitter
.com/redcross) provide information and disaster-related
updates.**

Red Cross volunteers are able to send an SMS about a new shelter
opening or the changing direction of a brushfire and have lots of
people read it at the same time.

But Twitter also brings the benefit of immediate feedback—and
that can have tremendous advantages for individuals.

The Power of Twitter's Immediate Feedback

Twitter's speed means that you can send out an SMS to Twitter from
wherever you are and have lots of people read it immediately. That's
a service that was really meant for fun, but it's proven itself to be
hugely valuable as a way of asking for help.

In June 2008, Pastor Carlos Whittaker (twitter.com/loswhit), Service Programming Director at Buckhead Church in Atlanta, Georgia,
found himself stuck at the airport in Dallas and was told he would
have to wait six hours for the next flight. Tired and not too happy at
the thought of spending a night on the airport floor, he sent a tweet
about his predicament.

Within just two minutes, he had received seven e-mails, three
phone calls, and a huge number of tweets.

Best of all, Trevor DeVage of charity group Remedy4ThisHeart turned up and gave Carlos a key to a room at a nearby Hyatt hotel.

That was certainly a helpful response, but sometimes tweets can generate the sort of response that makes an even more important difference to people's lives.

In April 2008, for example, James Buck (twitter.com/jamesbuck), a journalism student at the University of California at Berkeley, was arrested with his interpreter, Mohammed Maree, while photographing an anti-government rally in Egypt. Sitting in the police van, he was able to use his mobile phone to send the one-word message "arrested" to his followers on Twitter. They immediately alerted the U.S. embassy and his college, which quickly obtained a lawyer for him. James continued to provide updates about his arrest via Twitter, and was released the following day, which he announced on Twitter with the word "free."

His interpreter was less lucky: Maree was held for 90 days, beaten and abused, and was only released after a hunger strike.

Both of those examples relied on Twitter followers taking action outside Twitter. But that's not usually where the responses take place.

One of the most enjoyable aspects of Twitter isn't updating friends and family about the small details of your life. That's fun, but it only works one way.

Twitter is a two-way communication tool—and that's very important.

Figure 2.5 The tweet that freed journalism student, James Buck, from an Egyptian jail.

It means you can ask questions and request help to very specialized problems, and get the expert advice you need.

Instant Access to Smart People 24/7

Later in this book, I'm going to talk in more detail about how to use Twitter not just as a billboard for making announcements, but as way of holding a conversation with people who matter.

Usually, you'll be holding that conversation with friends or customers. But because Twitter has such a well-educated and professional group of followers, it can also function as an always-open help center for just about any subject you can imagine.

Look at people's Twitter pages and you'll see this time and time again.

Hidden among the announcements about the type of music they're listening to or the work they're doing, you'll see questions

Realtime results for anyone know   0.11 seconds

howlatthemoon: Does **anyone** on my twitter list **know** who Timothy Claypole is? Rent-a-ghost?
half a minute ago · Reply · View Tweet

neilang: I've resorted to using an old Dell. **Anyone know** of a good Rails IDE for Vista?
3 minutes ago · Reply · View Tweet

armorgan: **Anyone know** when DST is?
13 minutes ago · Reply · View Tweet

seancarmody: Just watching an old clip of the Rolling Stone's Sympathy for the Devil. **Anyone know** who the blonde guy on the maracas is?
31 minutes ago · Reply · View Tweet

aditya: **Anyone know** of a ScriptDoc parser for TextMate? Or just one in general?
about 1 hour ago · Reply · View Tweet

Figure 2.6   A random search at search.twitter.com for the keyword phrase "anyone know" suggests that a call for help— or at least a call like this—goes out on Twitter about every 10 minutes.

about how to fix this problem, where they can buy that gizmo, or even what they should have for supper. (Twitter users do seem to think about food a lot!)

Some of those questions are a bit silly. Some, though, are very technical, but Twitter can actually answer them.

The answer to Aditya's question about a ScriptDoc parser for TextMate, for example, appears to have been JSDoc.

If you want to know what that is, don't ask me; ask someone on Twitter.

So that's the history and that's where Twitter came from. It's an incredibly simple tool that has already had a massive impact on people's lives. Growing out of social media sites to focus on just one tiny action, it's become hugely popular with some of the world's smartest people and highest earners. It's pulled innocents out of prison and given a lost pastor a place to sleep.

It's useful, it's important, and it can generate earnings for any business, online or offline. But you have to know how to use it. In the rest of this book, I'm going to reveal all of the most important tips, strategies, and approaches for getting the most out of Twitter.

It's going to be hands-on, practical, comprehensive, and results-driven.

So let's start right at the beginning.

3

Getting Started the Right Way on Twitter

A large part of Twitter's beauty is its simplicity. Sign up to many of the other social networking sites and you'll be asked questions about your life that cover everything from where you went to school to your favorite color.

On Twitter, people are happy to let everyone know what they had for lunch (as well as breakfast, supper, brunch, afternoon snack, and what they dunked in their coffee) but that's not because Twitter asks them to.

In fact, the site keeps everything very clean and easy to use.

In this chapter, I'm going to help you get to grips with the basics of Twitter. It's not difficult to understand, but you will need to know the way the site works and how to use it. I'll explain what happens during registration, what followers and tweets are, and how to send and receive those all-important messages.

Signing Up—Does Twitter Have the Web's Most Friendly Registration Page?

At some point, every Internet entrepreneur is going to face a dilemma. They look at Google's home page with its white space and single line search box and they realize that simple is good.

29

Figure 3.1   Membership of Twitter is free . . . but restricted to humans.

Then they look at the list of all the features they want their site to include and they stuff their home page and their registration page—and every other page—with features and information that only a fraction of their users will want and only a few people will ever use.

It's just too tempting, and it's a mistake that gums up the works of businesses as varied as dating services and networking sites.

Twitter didn't make that mistake. Hit the big green button on their home page—you can't miss it—and you'll be taken to a sign-up page thtat has just three fields: username, password, and e-mail address.

You'll also be asked to enter a couple of words to prove that you're human.

It couldn't be simpler, could it?

Well actually, this is where simple can be bad.

It's the first place you can make a mistake.

Your username isn't just a phrase you're going to enter when you sign in. It will form part of your URL and will be visible whenever you promote your Twitter page.

It's like a choosing a domain name for a Web site. Choose poorly, and you could affect your Twitter account's ability to gather followers and build a reputation.

Your username might be the first thing you enter, but it should be an item you think about deeply.

Your full name is a possibility, provided it hasn't been taken already, but another good option is to use your Web site's domain name. That would link your site together with your Twitter account and make clear that the one is just a natural extension of the other.

Whatever you choose, just make sure that it's:

1. Closely associated with you.

The formula "twitter.com/username" makes finding people on Twitter very easy. If you don't want to search around for someone, you can just pop their name after "twitter.com" and see if they're there.

It's very easy and it means you can have hours of (almost) endless fun. Try surfing to twitter.com/billgates, for example, or twitter.com/stevejobs. Or toss in any other celebrity you can think of and try to figure out which are real Twitterers.

But people are only going to be able to use this easy URL facility to find you if your username is a phrase that's closely associated with you.

That's made even more important by Twitter's onsite search engine, which is very precise. While Facebook's search engine will return suggestions and near-misses if it can't find an exact match, Twitter will just tell you that it can't find that person.

If you pick a random username, you leave a valuable advantage on the table.

2. Easy to remember.

If a username is closely associated with you, it should be easy to remember, but that isn't always the case. Opt for something long to make it stand out, and you'll increase the

Figures 3.2 and 3.3   This is the username that I chose for my
Twitter page...and this is how it appears in the browser. Creative?
Nope. Memorable and easy to find? Absolutely!

> chances that even a small typo will send potential followers
> the wrong way.
>
> Tossing in numbers as a way of keeping a version of
> common name to yourself works fine in passwords, but as a
> username that's going to form part of your URL, it's a strict
> no-no.
>
> Keep it short, simple to remember, and closely associated
> with who you are and what you do.

You can change your Twitter URL, but if you're going to do that,
you should do it good and early. Creating a new name after you've
already created a long list of followers is something you should really
try to avoid.

Who's on Twitter? Your First Followers!

Once you've picked a username, entered a password, and proven
that you're a human being and not a robot bent on sending everyone
spam, you'll begin a three-step process that will start you following
people on Twitter.

None of these steps takes more than a minute or two, but the
good news is that you can skip them if you want to.

The even better news is that you *should* skip these steps, at least
for now.

The first step is to search any online mail service that you
use—such as Hotmail, Yahoo!, and Gmail—to see whether anyone
with the e-mail addresses listed in your address book has already
registered an account at Twitter.

Figure 3.4 You can start searching on Twitter even before you've created your profile. But you should probably create your profile first.

The second step is to start following anyone in your address book who is already on the site.

And the third step presents you with a giant list containing everyone in your address book who isn't on Twitter, so that you can send them an invitation to join the site.

It means that you can start following your friends and contacts right away. And it means too that you can bring in everyone you know so that they're following you.

So why do I think you should skip this stage when you sign up?

Because the most powerful way to win followers on Twitter is to follow them yourself.

If you start following people on Twitter, they'll receive a message saying that you're following them.

They'll then come to your Twitter page, and at this stage of your registration what will they see?

Nothing.

You haven't uploaded a picture yet. You haven't designed your Twitter page yet.

You haven't even issued a tweet yet!

Why would anyone choose to follow a Twitterer with a profile like that?

Being able to see which of your friends and contacts are already on Twitter—and follow them all right away—is such a valuable tool that you shouldn't waste it until your own profile is ready.

Until then, it's going to be more valuable for Twitter, which will pick up referrals to everyone on your contact list, than to you.

You will be able to come back to this later when your profile is ready, so my advice would be to skip this step for now, and....

Create an Inviting Twitter Profile

Skip the instant searching and you'll be taken right into your profile.

At this stage, there won't be much to see. You'll have the default blue background. Your profile image will consist of the default brown square with the odd "o_O" logo inside. And you'll have no followers, you'll be following no one, and you'll have no updates.

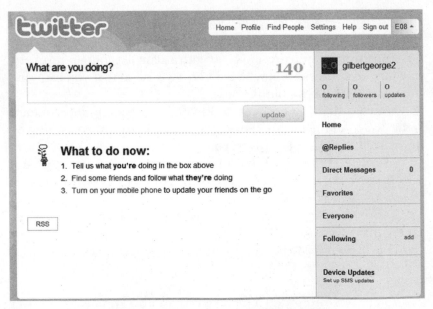

Figure 3.5 A brand new Twitter profile. Think of it as a blank canvas on which you're about to create a marketing masterpiece and start at the very top, not the bottom.

What you will have, though, is a box in which you can make your first tweet, and a list of things that Twitter thinks you should do next.

You shouldn't do any of those things next. You certainly shouldn't start by telling "us what you're doing in the box above."

Who's "us"?

Certainly not the people at Twitter. They aren't going to read every first tweet sent by every new Twitterer.

And certainly not your followers. You don't have any! Sending a tweet at this stage won't do you any harm, but it won't do you any good either. No one will read it.

gilbertgeorge2

| Account | Password | Devices | Notices | Picture | Design |

Name: gilbertgeorge2
Enter your real name, so people you know can recognize you.

Username: gilbertgeorge2   Your URL: http://twitter.com /gilbertgeorge2
No spaces, please.

Email:

Time Zone: (GMT-03:00) Greenland

More Info URL:
Have a homepage or a blog? Put the address here. (You can also add Twitter to your site here)

One Line Bio:
About yourself in fewer than 160 chars.

Location:
Where in the world are you?

Language: English
What language would you like to Twitter in?

☐ Protect my updates
Only let people whom I approve follow my updates. If this is checked, you WILL NOT be on the public timeline.

Save

Account
From here you can change your basic account info, fill in your profile data, and set whether you want to be private or public.

Tips

- Filling in your profile information will help people find you on Twitter. For example, you'll be more likely to turn up in a Twitter search if you've added your location or your real name.

- Change your Twitter user name anytime without affecting your existing updates, @replies, direct messages, or other data. After changing it, make sure to let your followers know so you'll continue receiving all of your messages with your new user name.

- Protect your profile to keep your Twitter updates private. Approve who can follow you and keep your updates out of search results.

Figure 3.6 What Twitter calls "settings" actually offers a lot more than technical choices. It's one of the most important pages for successful Twitter marketing.

Or at least no one will read it until they've started follow-ing you. At that time, they'll be free to see the first tweet you uploaded—which, because you just did it to see what this tweeting thing is all about, might not be very interesting at all.

It's a bit like uploading a random Web page just to see what creating a Web page is like—and then leaving it up for all future users to see.

Forget about sending tweets for now.

Don't worry about finding some friends to follow.

And you certainly don't need to concern yourself about turning on your mobile to update your friends while you're on the go.

Instead, click the *Settings* link at the top of the page and give yourself a proper profile.

You'll be presented with a form that looks a lot like the sort of forms you're used to filling in on social media sites. You'll have a list of questions to answer that look simple, but actually require a little thought.

Name and Username

It starts with your name.

Yes, you should know your name, and that question shouldn't be hard. But it might be.

You probably have more than one name. You have a name. Your Web site might have a name. Your business might have a completely different name.

And that's assuming you just have one business and one Web site.

I've already pointed out the importance of choosing a username that can be typed directly into the browser. That's vital, and even though it's going to appear at the top of your profile page, it's never going to be pretty.

Because it's also a URL, whatever phrase you choose is going to appear as one word.

Your "name" will appear on the right of your Twitter page and reveals who you *really* are.

So before you type in your name, *you have to decide which brand you want your Twitter page to represent.*

Will the tweets be about what *you're* doing now or will they be about what your company or Web site is doing now?

Do you see the difference?

My followers tend to be people who want tips and advice about Internet marketing. When they look for that advice, they don't turn to my company, Infomedia. They look for me.

My Twitter profile, therefore, uses both my username and my real name, so that I'm easy to find and so that anyone reading my tweets understands that they're coming directly from me.

They're getting information that they can trust.

Note that on the right of this page, Twitter points out that you can change your username without affecting the tweets and messages you've already sent and received.

That doesn't mean you should just enter the first username you think of.

Although your current store of messages will be safe, you will have to tell your followers about the change. When you've got a lot of followers—and if you use the strategies in the next chapter, you *will* have a lot of followers—that's always going to be a real pain.

In fact, one good strategy when you join Twitter is to open multiple accounts so that you can tweet about different subjects on different timelines. Twitter doesn't allow cybersquatting—and Twitterers who have tried it have had their accounts suspended—but if you think you might need more than one account, then it's worth reserving your usernames sooner rather than later.

Twitter is becoming a popular place!

E-MAIL

Your choice of name and username isn't going to be too difficult. If you have more than one identity or brand, it might take a little thought but usually, the choice should be fairly clear.

Your choice of e-mail is a lot easier.

This isn't an e-mail address that anyone is going to see. If people want to contact you through Twitter, they'll have to do it either by replying to one of your tweets or by sending you a direct message. But they won't see your e-mail address.

The address you enter here will only be used to receive information such as Twitter's newsletters and to change your password.

If you're the kind of person who tends to forget passwords, that second use can be pretty helpful! Make sure that you choose an e-mail address that you actually use.

TIME ZONE

Time on the Internet tends to be a pretty strange thing. Check your e-mail client and you might find all sorts of strange times attached to the e-mails you've received; often they look like they have no relationship at all to the time the message was sent.

Usually, that doesn't matter at all.

On Twitter though, because tweets describe what you're doing *now*, time is important.

So for the most recent posts, Twitter displays how long ago the tweets were sent. If a tweet is a day old though, the time stamp refers to the time the tweet was sent based on the time zone *the follower* entered on the settings page.

I think that's a bit confusing. I'd rather know what time of day the person I'm following sent his tweets.

Again, it's not a hard question, but I think this is one that Twitter got wrong.

#Elevate 2008 is over! A truly amazing event and I'm now ready for vacation :-)
about 7 hours ago from web

Did you miss Saturday Night Live from Elevate 2008? The replay is now available! http://tinyurl.com/62elhh *1:30 AM yesterday from web*

30 minutes to Elevate LIVE! There's never been a live show like this... http://tinyurl.com/jclive 10 pm EDT, 7 pm PDT! *10:27 PM Oct 25th from web*

Figure 3.7 Three different kinds of time stamp on my tweets as seen by a follower. One of them was right, but at least they're in the right order—and that's what counts!

MORE INFO URL

And now we come to something that's really crucial.

Twitter's profile appears to provide space to promote just one Web site. In fact, as I'll point out later in this section, with a little creativity, it's possible to promote all the Web sites you want.

But even then, one Web site—the link that appears beneath your name on the right of the screen—will always be the most prominent. It's the one that people will click to find out exactly who you are and what lies behind this Twitterer.

That makes the link very, very powerful.

Usually, you'll want to link to your main Web site. Sometimes though, you might want to change this link to suit a particular promotion. If you were promoting a new e-book or affiliate product, for example, you could tweet about it on Twitter and link from your profile to a landing page. Your tweets then would become another channel to bring potential buyers to your store.

Do you see how useful this can be?

ONE-LINE BIO

So far, all of the fields I've discussed have been very, very simple.

They're very important—and you should know that they're much more important than they look—but none of them should have you scratching your head for more than a few seconds.

Your bio will take some effort, and a fair bit of thought, too.

Writing about yourself is never much fun. That's especially true when you're doing it for business. You have to find the things in your life that are interesting to others, make yourself appear professional, and do it all without boasting or sounding vain.

Usually, that's pretty hard.

Twitter makes it a real challenge—it only gives you 160 characters.

That's right, you get just 20 more characters than you have to write a tweet to describe your entire life history.

What a relief!

That means you can't go into detail, talk about all the things you've done and what you do for others. All you can do is choose

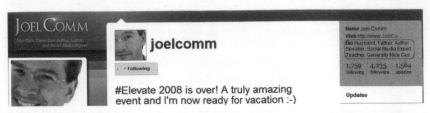

Figure 3.8 My bio as it used to appear on Twitter. Should I include my location here? Maybe, but it's not critical and might localize my brand too much.

one or two of the most important facts about you and write a sentence.

As an example, for a long time, my bio used to say:

"Husband, Father. Author. Speaker, Social Media Expert, Teacher. Generally Nice Guy."

You could follow exactly the same model, or you could produce your own. If you published a sports Web site, for example, you could write something like:

"Football fan, youth coach, and all-round sports nut with bad knees."

That's a very simple format: three one- or two-word phrases that describe who you are or what you do, followed by a short joke to finish it off.

If you wanted to create a bio like this, you don't have to do any more than fill in these blanks:

"[Professional description 1], [Professional description 2] and [Professional description 3] who likes to [Personal description.]"

A professional photographer looking to use Twitter to promote his services then, could easily use that format to create a bio that said:

"Wedding photographer, portrait pro, and creative artist who likes to photograph his kids at embarrassing moments."

A landscape contractor could come up with a bio that looks like this:

"Tree surgeon, garden expert and green-fingered designer who likes to smell freshly-cut grass."

And someone who blogs about sport could use that format to create this bio:

"Lakers fan, Yankees nut, and fantasy football coach who likes to tailgate downwind of the barbecues."

Do you see how bios like these leave room for just two or three basic facts about you while still allowing space for a little personal touch? That's all you have room for on Twitter, and it's all you need.

If people want to find out more they'll have to come to your Web site. (I told you that link was going to be important!)

So one way of writing your Twitter bio is to summarize yourself in 160 characters. That's the approach I've chosen and it's a very simple one.

An alternative approach is to write a bio that discusses a particular project.

This is a very different use of Twitter. Instead of tweeting about yourself in general, you'll be tweeting on one theme—which you can then change when that project ends.

British comedy actor and writer Stephen Fry (twitter.com/stephenfry), for example, is known for being tech-savvy. He has a Web site that he updates frequently and on which he blogs, vlogs, and podcasts. He also tweets several times a day, even when he's working.

He probably does that mostly because he enjoys it—tweeting is fun, after all—but there's no question that his tweets also help to generate interest in his latest projects so that when they're released, they already have an audience.

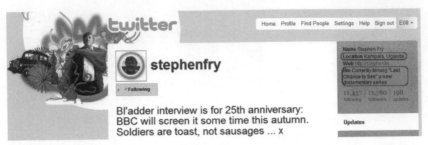

Figure 3.9 With almost 12,000 followers, British celebrity Stephen Fry is one of Twitter's top users. Look at how he uses his bio and his current location to promote his latest project.

In the fall of 2008, for example, the BBC sent Stephen Fry around the world to film a documentary series about endangered animals. Fry constantly changed his location to reflect where he was tweeting from and updated his bio to describe what he was doing at the time.

His tweets still helped to promote his personal brand. They were still about what he was doing at the time (and yes, that included descriptions of what he was eating for breakfast at the hotel). But because the bio placed them in the context of a large project, those tweets were easier for new followers to understand, and *they had a very strong promotional effect.*

This is something that any marketer could do.

A photographer sent to Alaska for a week to shoot oil wells could change the location on his bio to reflect where he is now, and alter his bio to:

"Currently shooting oil wells in Alaska for Shell."

A landscape contractor could edit his bio to describe a big project he's been hired to complete:

"Now designing the flowerbeds for Ventura's new Ben Sheffer Park."

And someone who was writing an e-book about fantasy football could write this in his bio:

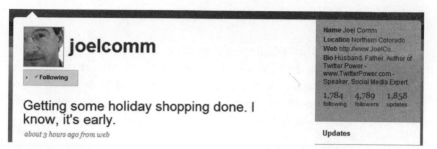

Figure 3.10 My current bio, which includes information about this book.

> *"Now working on the ultimate guide to real success with fantasy football."*

Since putting this book together, for example, I've changed my bio to emphasize my work with Twitter.

Bios like these look like tweets themselves—but they're not.

Tweets describe what you're doing at one particular moment. They can't describe what you're doing over a period that lasts days, weeks, or months. Your bio can do that, and when it does, it focuses your tweets onto that one project.

When you have a lot of followers, it can be a very powerful way of promoting your work.

LOCATION

After asking you to sum up your life in 160 characters, Twitter then asks "Where in the world are you?"

We've already seen how changing your location to reflect where you happen to be working on a particular project can be very helpful.

Usually though, you'll be working in the same place most of the time, so you should be a little careful here.

I don't try to hide the fact that I live in Loveland, Colorado. In fact, I talk about it quite a lot on my blog. It's a beautiful place and I feel very blessed that I'm able to live here.

But my products have nothing to do with my location. When I attend conferences, I meet people from around the country, and

I know that my books, courses, and products are used by people around the world.

I don't think that placing my location on my bio would really affect my branding, but I don't want people to feel that my work is somehow connected to Colorado. It isn't, so I chose to leave it off.

If there's a chance that your location could localize your work, then you might want to leave the location off, too.

PROTECT MY UPDATES

I'll skip the language setting because that's pretty self-explanatory. The last option on this page, though, is perhaps the most important of all.

Twitter's last question is whether you want to keep your tweets confidential so that only the people you approve see them, or whether you're prepared to let anyone at all see them.

If you're using Twitter for marketing, do not click this box.

You want to let anyone who wants to see your tweets. You want as many people as possible to come to your Twitter page, realize that you have fantastic, interesting tweets that they want to read, and sign up to be your followers.

If people can't see your updates, they're not going to sign up. You'll be restricted to tweeting to the friends, family, and contacts that you've chosen.

That's like a store owner hanging a "closed" sign on the door and only dealing with her friends.

If you want to tweet only about personal stuff, that's fine. But it's a different use of Twitter. If you want to use Twitter to build your brand and grow your business, then leave that box unchecked.

Choosing Your Twitter Picture

All of your profile information is reached by clicking the *Settings* link at the top of the page, and is listed under the tab marked *Account*.

There are six *Settings* tabs all together, but for now I want to skip past the *Password*, *Devices*, and *Notices* settings, and continue with the tabs that relate to your profile—the way you'll appear to followers.

Figure 3.11 Twitter places your bio information under the Account tab and separates Picture and Design.

I believe that you should first prepare your page before you start sending and receiving tweets. Once you've completed your bio (and yes, you can change it later if you're not completely satisfied with it), your next step should be to upload a picture.

You *will* need to upload a picture to your Twitter profile.

There's no getting around this step.

If you don't add a photo to your profile, you'll appear on the page as two strange circles. That's not very attractive, and worst of all, it makes you look like you're not serious about your time on Twitter.

When people add their photos, they'll expect to see yours in return.

And it has to be a good picture too, one that portrays you as both professional and personable—exactly what your tweets should be doing.

Remember, though, that the picture itself is going to appear very small, so it's a good idea to use a close-up of your face that makes you recognizable, even when you're no bigger than a thumbnail. Try to include a full-body shot and your expression will probably appear no larger than a couple of millimeters on someone's screen.

You'll usually be better off with a good portrait that shows you smiling and at ease.

That's easier said than done, and in practice people make a lot of mistakes here.

Spend any time at all on social networking sites and you'll see photograph after photograph that look blurry or are just plain inappropriate. Here are number of guidelines to follow when adding your picture to any social media site, including Twitter:

♦ Don't hold the camera yourself.

    Showing your arm doesn't look cool. In fact, it looks like you couldn't find a friend to hold the camera for you, or you don't know how to work the camera's self-timer. Neither of those create good impressions—and neither creates good pictures either.

The pictures that I use on my social media sites have all been professionally shot. If you're serious about marketing with social media that's something you might want at least to consider too. You can either visit a local photography studio or use BetterBusinessShots.com, a service that will send you to a local hand-picked photographer who will shoot a selection of portraits specifically for online use at prices that start at $99.

Alternatively, you can just ask someone to lend you a hand so that you don't have to show your arm.

♦ Use a good camera.

Many laptops today come with built-in webcams. Desktop Web cameras are almost as standard as a keyboard and mouse, and even the cheapest mobile phone comes complete with a lens, e-mail facility, and practically a portable photography studio, too.

Don't use them.

Cameras like these tend to produce low-quality images with lots of distortion. They're hard to focus and often produce images that are grainy rather than clear.

If you want to video conference with a friend or a business partner on the other side of the country, your webcam will do a fine job. I use mine all the time.

If you want to snap your friends at a birthday dinner, your mobile phone is just the ticket.

But when you're creating a portrait that will represent you on a social media site, use a real camera. Nothing else is good enough.

♦ Keep the backgrounds to a minimum.

Because you have such a tiny amount of space to squeeze your picture into, anything in the background is going to interfere with the most important item in the frame: you.

Ideally, your features should fill most of the frame. And behind you, there should be just about nothing.

You might be able to get away with a horizon line, the sea, or the sky but if the background is busy in any way—if it shows trees, parts of buildings, or your car—it's going to distract from your portrait and look unfocused.

Find a nice white wall or a good high balcony and stand your friend, with the camera, directly in front of you.

♦ Show yourself.

And finally, use *your* picture, not a photograph of your cat, your dog, your hamster, your favorite comic book hero, or some squiggle that you feel might do a good job of representing you.

If you're tweeting on behalf of your company, then you can get away with using your company logo. Other than that though, you'll need to use your photograph.

Social media is all about personal branding. It's about the connections you build as an individual and how you work that network.

To create those connections, you can't be a wallflower. You need to show your face. So shy or not, you need to upload a picture to your profile.

And it has to be a good one!

Designing Your Twitter Profile

Now we really get down to business.

When it comes to choosing your profile picture, there's really only one option. You want to make it a close-up of your face, and make it fill the frame so that no one has to squint to look at you.

Your profile design, though, is a lot more complicated.

I've pointed out that Twitter leaves you very little room for creativity in your bio. You're not going to be able to say too much when you only have 160 characters.

And the site is very tightfisted with the links too. Most of us have more than one site we'd like to promote, and it would also be good to bring Twitter's users into our Facebook network, Flickr streams, and MySpace pages. Being forced to place just one link on your profile is like taking a kid to a candy store and telling him he can only choose one piece of candy.

Why restrict your followers to just one marketing channel?

Figure 3.12   Twitter's profile design options are a lot more
flexible—and much more useful—than they look.

The background image gives you a chance to have it all.
But you'll have to do a bit of planning.

Twitter gives you a selection of twelve background images to
choose from.

You don't want to choose any of them. You want to create your
own background and upload it by clicking the *Change background
image* link beneath Twitter's designs.

Instead of leaving the left side of your Twitter page blank or filled
with some strange design, you want to use that space to promote
your business.

That strip is valuable real estate, and not using it as good as
leaving money on the table.

This what my Twitter profile looks like. Take a look at the
left side of the screen. You can think of it as having four separate
sections.

The first section is the top-left hand corner. This is where the
page begins so it needs to function as an introduction. It should say
who you are and indicate with a glance what you do.

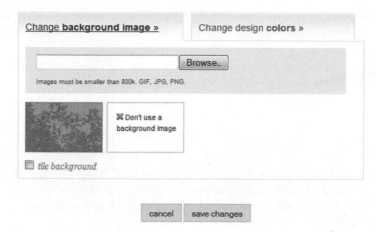

Figure 3.13 Change your background image and start building on your Twitter real estate.

On my profile, I've done that with a stylized version of my name and a descriptive tag line. You could also put your logo here.

Remember that unlike a conventional Web page, this won't be the first place the user will look. Your latest tweet will always be far

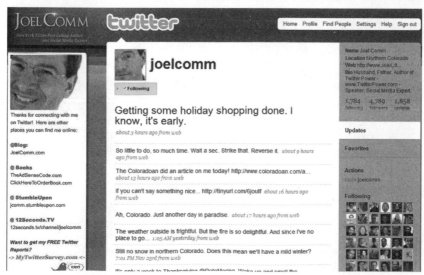

Figure 3.14 My specially constructed Twitter background explains who I am, promotes my sites and my books, and sends people to my Twitter survey. What will yours do?

more prominent and draw the eye first. The user will then look at the top left-hand corner in order to be able to see at a glance who is providing these tweets.

That means this corner should contain an image or text that's visually enticing and which draws the viewer down the column.

Directly beneath that, I've created an information column.

This is just a vertical bar that runs alongside my tweets and tells my followers basic information about me and—even more importantly—where they can go to find out more.

At the top of the sidebar, I've placed a second picture of myself.

You don't have to place a picture there if you don't want to. It depends on the nature of your business and what you're promoting with Twitter.

If you're promoting your personal brand, then using an image that's larger than the tiny box provided for your profile can be very helpful.

People will see your profile thumbnail on someone else's Twitter page then click it to see who you are. They'll reach your profile and by seeing a second photo will feel that they're getting more than the simple introduction the thumbnail provides. They'll feel that they're getting a peek behind the scenes of your business.

If you're promoting a product or a brand though, you could place a picture of that product here, or simply go straight into the text on the information bar.

That begins with a brief introduction. One option is to explain what followers will receive if they continue reading your tweets.

An introduction like this provides information about the benefits of becoming a follower, says something about what you do, and also functions as a "call to action," encouraging people to hit that *Follow* button.

Follow me and learn as I tweet about *marketing, social media* and *much more*.

Figure 3.15 An invitation and a further introduction.

Thanks for connecting with me
on Twitter! Here are other
places you can find me online:

Figure 3.16   My sidebar, complete with
connections to my other Web spaces.

You can use the same format in your own information bar. If you wanted your Twitter page to promote a blog about your travel experiences, you could write:

"Follow me as I travel the world, visit ancient sites and eat some very strange food."

It's very simple and it can be very effective.

An alternative approach is to do something even simpler. You can thank the user for following you and send him off to learn more about you. That's the approach I now take in my sidebar.

What could possibly be easier than that?

The bulk of the information bar is just a list of links that tell followers where they can go to discover more. Again, this is very simple, *but it could well be the most important part of your Twitter presence.*

You can have all the followers you want. You could have tens of thousands of people reading your tweets every day and telling all their friends about you. But if that's all they do, they're going to be of no use to you.

You need them to come to your other Web sites. You need them to click your ads, purchase your products, or subscribe to your services.

You need them to help you make money—and that's not going to happen directly on Twitter. It can only happen by sending them to your other sites.

This sidebar is the place to tell them where they can find those sites.

Note how I provide lots of different options, and how I use headings to make the differences between those options clear.

This is a very different strategy from one that you might be using on your Web site. There, you're more likely to use just a few external links so that you can control where your users go and so that those links don't compete with your ads.

Here's the secret...

Your sidebar is actually an ad. It functions just like a Google AdSense unit—but it's your Google AdSense unit.

AdSense is probably the most used advertising network on the Internet. Operated by Google, the system's ads, delivered automatically and contextualized to match the page content, are what turned the search engine company into a multibillion-dollar corporation.

And I'm pleased to say that I, and thousands of others, have enjoyed a great deal of success with them. I wrote about strategies and techniques for using Google's multi-billion dollar ad program at length in my previous title, The AdSense Code (2006—Morgan James Publishing.)

You can't put AdSense units on your Twitter page. But you can create your very own AdSense-type unit that promotes you.

The design is different, but the principle is exactly the same. You're tweets are your content—good content, of course—and the

@Blog:
JoelComm.com

@ Books
TheAdSenseCode.com
ClickHereToOrderBook.com

@ StumbleUpon
jcomm.stumbleupon.com

@ 12Seconds.TV
12seconds.tv/channel/joelcomm

Figure 3.17 It's not AdSense, but it works like AdSense...almost.

ad runs alongside it. Naturally, it looks nothing like an ad so that people actually want to look at it, not run away from it.

That's the foundation of smart AdSense implementation, and it works in exactly the same way with these homemade "ads" on Twitter.

And just as an AdSense unit usually includes lots of different links, so that readers have a choice and are likely to find at least one of them interesting, so your sidebar is more likely to tempt your readers if it's filled with lots of different URLs.

So the headings tell people what sort of content they can find on those sites, and directly beneath those headings are the URLs themselves.

There is however one very important difference between your Twitter sidebar and an AdSense unit:

You can't click the links in your sidebar.

It's just an image. It doesn't do anything except provide a background to your tweet timeline.

Clearly, that's a huge weakness. You can do something to get around it with some smart design work. I've made the headings and keywords in my information bar blue so that they look like links.

They might not function as links, but they will be as eye-catching as links.

Note that I didn't make the URLs themselves blue. That would be misleading. Followers might want to click them, and they'd be irritated when they find that they can't.

The best I can do to help guide them to my Web sites is to make the heading stand out in standard link blue, and create enough curiosity with my tweets to make followers type the URL into the browser to learn more.

And finally, at the bottom of the page, I've highlighted one particular link that I would really like my Twitter users to follow. In this case, it's my Twitter survey—much of the information from which went into this book.

But the beauty of that last section of the information bar is that it can change.

Whenever you want to promote a new product, all you have to do is edit your background image and change the information about the product page.

Figure 3.18   The bottom of my information bar gives a final kick to my promotions.

If you're thinking that I should have put that promotion at the top of my information bar, then think again.

Your most important product should go at the top of the information bar—the brand that you want most to promote. In the case of my Twitter page, that's my personal brand.

My Twitter page isn't about my Twitter survey. It's about me, so my brand goes at the top of the page. The Twitter survey is the second most important item I'd like to promote, so that goes at the bottom of the page, together with an image, so that it stands out.

Simple!

Designing a Commercial Background Image for Twitter

Or rather the design is simple, because creating your background image can be a little technical.

It's not *very* technical but if, like me, you know absolutely nothing about graphic design you might want to outsource the image production itself to a professional designer.

Supply the mock-up, explain what you want the image to include, and let the designer do the hard work of making sure all the figures add up—because your design will need to have all the right dimensions if it's going to succeed.

Hugh Briss, for example, offers customized Twitter backgrounds through his Web site, TwitterImage.com. Prices start from $75, and he's already created beautiful backgrounds for some of Twitter's biggest users, including Chris Pirillo (twitter.com/chrispirillo) and blogging expert Darren Rowse (twitter.com/problogger).

That's the easiest option. But actually, there are a whole bunch of different ways of creating a background image for Twitter, and some of them are very easy indeed.

If I can do it, no one has an excuse!

1. Do it all yourself.

The hard way is to open up Photoshop (or Gimp or Paint.Net, if you prefer to use a simpler graphics program that doesn't cost anything) and get designing.

Here's what you need to know:

o The maximum size for the image is 800kb.

o The image dimensions can be flexible. Mine is 1898 × 1593, which is standard and does the job. Stretching it to 2048 × 1707, though, would make sure it fills even the biggest screens.

o The dimensions of the sidebar on the left are 80 pixels × 587 pixels.

o The top of the Twitter logo is 14 pixels from the top of the page. Place the highest point of your first image on the same line and it will be level with the logo.

Note that while you can put a sidebar—or anything else—on the right side of the page too, there's no guarantee that it will appear on screens with different sizes; on small screens, it could be hidden by the Twitter timeline. If you're putting the sidebar on the left, adding information on the right might also be distracting: you just want your users to see your links and your tweets, then surf on to find more. Hugh Briss, though, has come up with some pretty neat designs that use both sides of the screen.

If you've got skills with colors, shapes, and design programs, then you can use these figures to get creative. If you don't, you can keep things simple.

2. Use a free template.

Twitterer Wayne Sutton (twitter.com/waynesutton) has uploaded a free template that anyone can download and use as a foundation for their own backgrounds.

You can download the template file from Box.net at www.box.net/shared/lgw2pz4gso. Having saved the file, you'll be able to open it and start making the changes you want to the picture and the text.

That will give you the sidebar, but it won't give you a unique background design for the rest of the page. Fortunately there are a number of ways to deal with that, too.

3. Use a free background design.

Designer Natalie Jost (twitter.com/natalie) is giving away a bunch of beautiful background patterns at TwitterPatterns .com. You can only use them on your Twitter page—so no using them on your Web site without paying Natalie for her work first—but there are some beautiful choices there.

Alternatively, GrungeTextures.com also offers a big selection of textures and backgrounds that you can use under a Creative Commons license.

4. Use my background as a template.

Want to see what someone's background image looks like without all of the Twitter stuff on it?

Right click anywhere on the Twitter page and you'll be given a list of menu items. One of those menu items is "View background image."

Figure 3.19   Natalie Jost's Twitterpatterns.com provides a huge range of beautiful background designs—and all for free!

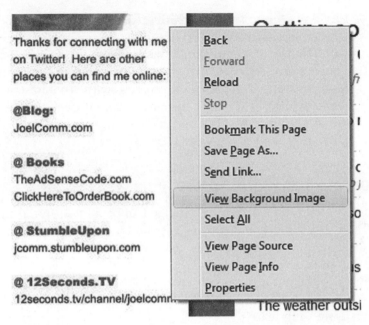

Figure 3.20   Removing the tweets from my Twitter page.

Press that option and you'll see a small version of the background image that was used to create someone's Twitter page. You can then expand the image to see it in real size.

Usually, you can only do this to get ideas. Other Twitterers aren't going to like you swiping their designs and building over them, but I don't mind. Feel free to use my background image as a template for your own.

You should change the background design itself—you don't want your page to look exactly like mine! And you should change the design of the logo, too, to match your own brand. But the sizing and dimensions will help to make sure that your background is exactly the right shape and size.

Finally, don't "tile" your background image. When you're including a sidebar, the result could be unusual—and not very pretty. It's a much better idea to make sure that your image is wide enough to fill the entire screen without being tiled.

5. Pay a designer to get it done right.

Just like with Web site design, you'll want to make sure your Twitter background looks professional. Several new services are popping up to help you accomplish this goal. Most recently, I've been impressed with Twitart (twitter.com/twitart). They will design a custom background and avatar for under $100. You can check out their portfolio and current pricing at www.TwitArt.com.

Choosing the Right Colors

Creating a tempting background image can be a lot of fun. It might look a little technical, and if you really find it daunting—or want to get something truly unique—you should be able to find a designer who can build something for you.

But it's really not necessary. You should be able to knock out something very effective within about half an hour, especially if you're using a template.

Figure 3.21 Colors are an important part of your Twitter design success. You can choose from a color wheel or type the code numbers in manually.

Twitter, though, also lets you choose your color scheme, and this can be a little tricky. The most important thing to bear in mind here is clarity.

You want your users to be able to read the text and find the links without having to squint, search, or generally become frustrated.

You can set the colors for five of the elements on your Twitter page: background, text, links, bio sidebar, and sidebar border.

BACKGROUND

If you've created your own background image—and, of course, you should have done—then you won't need to worry about this setting. The color will only appear on the right of the screen where your image ends.

Again, be sure to make the image large enough to fill even the biggest screen and this color won't be visible.

Just to be safe though, it's probably best to choose a color that matches the color of your background image. You'd lose any design, but the fact that your image is too narrow will be less obvious.

TEXT

The text setting refers only to the color of the words on the sidebar on the right. The Twitter timeline itself will always be black text on a white background.

Unless you've got some fantastic design in mind, make the text black—or some other dark color—and the background of the sidebar a relatively light color, so the text stands out.

Remember that design on the Web is all about results, not effects. You can have the most beautiful color combinations in the world, but if no one can read what you've written or can find your links, the design has failed.

LINKS

And that's why your links should always be blue.

Just use the default color that Twitter provides for this setting. It should be absolutely clear to your followers that the reference to your Web site is a link and that they can click it to learn more about you.

Confuse them and you'll lose clicks—and possible sales too.

Bio Sidebar

I've already mentioned that your bio sidebar on the right should be a light color so that the text that describes your bio information stands out. But it also needs to complement the design of your background image, so this might require a bit of experimentation.

Gray works well, so if in doubt, choose that.

Sidebar Border

And finally, the color of the borders in the right sidebar is the least prominent color that will appear on the page. It runs around your bio sidebar and between each of the bio's sections.

In fact, you'll probably only notice it if you get it wrong. Choose something garish, like canary yellow, and you'll see what I mean.

The safest bet is often black, but it will really depend on how you've set up your design. Make the sidebar border the same color as the sidebar background and you can get rid of the border altogether—another good choice.

Creating the right background design on Twitter is hugely important. It's a vital opportunity not just to make your Twitter page look good but to broadcast some valuable marketing information too.

It's worth making the effort to get it right.

Sometimes, less is more.

David Lawrence is a friend of mine who is a rising celebrity. If you watch the NBC TV show Heroes, you'll recognize him as the creepy and evil puppet master, Eric Doyle.

I noticed that David was not using Twitter, and he became a convert with just a few short e-mails. In just two weeks' time, he shot up to over 600 followers. I'm sure he'll have thousands by the time some of you read this book.

David's design is quite simple, and evidence that you don't need a fancy design to stand out. You can follow David at twitter .com/dhlawrencexvii.

Figure 3.22 The puppet master controls your tweets. Beware!

As an aside, fascination with celebrity is nothing new. There are a slew of meta-Twitter sites popping up which let you keep tabs on celebrities and other notable personalities based on their niche.

For example, www.FamousTweet.com tracks a number of actors, television stars, sports stars, authors, and more, all on one page.

Want to know what those in Internet business are saying? www.MarketingTweet.com tracks those in the marketing world.

As Twitter becomes more populated, I would expect a number of niche-oriented trackers to pop up.

Notices to Notice

Once you've created your background image, you'll ready to start tweeting. Or almost ready, because there are just a couple more small things you still have to do.

The first is to set your notices. This lets you choose how often you want Twitter to notify you.

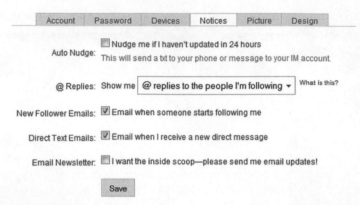

Figure 3.23 Twitter's notices can be a touch confusing.

If you let it, Twitter will notify you a lot. You want it to notify you sometimes, in ways that help you to build followers and enhance the site's marketing power.

Auto Nudge sends a text message to your phone or to your instant messaging account if you haven't sent a tweet in 24 hours. Frankly, I'd rather receive a message telling me I'm tweeting too much. Once you get started, that's a bigger danger than going a day without sending an update.

More important are the settings for @ *Replies*.

As we'll see, Twitter isn't just a place to broadcast your messages. It's also a place to have a conversation. People who see tweets are able to reply to them, ask questions, and answer queries.

This setting determines whether other people's responses to the tweets they read appear in your timeline, and if so, which people's.

You can choose between showing everyone's replies, only replies sent between people you're following, and showing no replies at all.

In general, you should choose to show everyone's replies.

Yes, that when you look at your home page you're going to see lots of messages that aren't directed at you. But you'll also see who is interested in the same sort of topics as you and who might make a potential follower—and a potential customer—in the future.

That's all valuable stuff.

When you want to have a lot of followers, showing all of their replies in your timeline can make a real difference.

You should also choose to receive e-mails when you pick up a *New Follower* and when someone sends you a *Direct Message*.

At some point, you might want to turn off those new follower notifications. If you're lucky enough to be getting dozens of new followers a day, it can get a bit annoying.

But you should keep your direct message e-mails. You won't receive too many of those, and you can choose either to ignore them or answer them. Either way, picking them up from your e-mail inbox is much more convenient than logging in to Twitter to do it.

And finally, receiving the *Twitter Newsletter* can be interesting—but not as interesting as reading the Twitter blog, which should become part of your regular Internet browsing. It's always full of useful stuff.

Turning On Your Devices

The last thing you should do before you start sending tweets is to set up your mobile phone.

Twitter began with mobiles in mind, so it's not too surprising that while you can have a lot of fun—and a lot of benefits—with Twitter just using your computer, being able to send and receive tweets from your mobile phone makes the whole experience much better.

You can send out an update while waiting for your meal in a restaurant, while you're standing in line at the DMV, or while you're sitting in the audience at a conference listening to a speaker—and sharing what you're hearing with your followers.

Figure 3.24 Twitter also lets you tweet to and from a mobile phone. You can be connected and computer-free.

It makes the whole thing much more convenient, and it means that you're much less likely to forget to update.

To send and receive tweets on your mobile, click the *Devices* tab under *Settings*, enter your phone number, and click the checkbox that allows you to receive tweets on your phone as SMS messages.

You'll then receive a code. Send that code to 40404 in the United States, 21212 in Canada, or +44 7624 801423 everywhere else, and your phone will be set up to send and receive tweets.

Because you've agreed to receive tweets on your mobile, though, you are at risk. When you're following lots of people—and to build up followers, you will need to follow lots of people—your phone will be going off all the time.

So before you start following people, send the word "stop" or "quit" from your mobile phone to Twitter's number. That will leave your phone set up to receive messages, but stop you receiving any messages at all.

Later, you can choose to follow selected Twitterers by sending the message "on username" (e.g., "on joelcomm") so that only the Twitterers you feel are the most important turn up in your phone.

That's just one of a bunch of useful commands that you can send

---

Twitter Mobile Commands

@username + message

Sends a tweet to another Twitterer. Your message appears as a reply in their timeline.

D username + message

Sends a private message to a Twitterer's device, and saves a copy in their Web archive.

WHOIS username

Lets you read a Twitterer's profile information.

GET username

Retrieves a Twitterer's latest tweet.

NUDGE username

Asks a Twitterer to post an update.

FAV username

Marks someone's most recent tweet as a favorite.

STATS

Lets you see how many followers you have and how many people you're following.

INVITE phone number

Sends an invitation to join Twitter by SMS to someone's mobile phone.

Figure 3.25   Twitter Mobile Commands

Figure 3.26 Love your tweet or hate it, once it's up, Twitter gives you options.

to Twitter from your mobile phone once it's set up to send and receive tweets.

And that's it!

Once you've done that, you're ready to send your first tweet.

Sending Your Very First Tweet

Hit the home link at the top of the page to return to your Twitter page.

There, at the top of the screen, is Twitter's constant question "What are you doing?" Beneath it is the space for you to write—in 140 characters—an answer.

So off you go.

Type whatever is going through your mind and hit "update."

Don't worry if you can't think of anything very smart and witty to write. At this stage, you just want try writing something so that you can see what happens. "Joining Twitter!" is good enough.

Now anyone will be able to read that tweet.

If that sounds like a terrible idea, click the tweet and you'll get a time stamp. Click that time stamp, and you'll get the tweet itself. On the right of the update will be two icons: a star and a trash can.

The star "faves" the tweet (marks it as a favorite) so that you can easily find it again. The trash can deletes the tweet. There's a good chance that you'll find both of those useful.

Becoming a Follower

The last thing you need to do before you're ready to start building up your Twitter presence is to follow people.

This is the easiest part of Twitter, and really the most enjoyable. There are so many amazing people on the site that you shouldn't have any trouble at all finding people whose tweets you want to read and who you want to follow.

If you already know who you want to follow on Twitter, just surf to their Twitter page and hit the *Follow* button. If not, there's a stack of people in the directory at the back of this book who post very interesting updates.

You're welcome to go to twitter.com/joelcomm and follow me too!

So that's the basics. You now know how to set up your Twitter account and create an attractive profile that acts as a marketing tool. And you know too how to send tweets and follow people.

Now you can start building up your own followers.

4

Building a Following on Twitter

Web sites have users, Facebook has friends, and Twitter has followers. They follow your messages—and in the process, they follow your life.

Unlike users or Facebook friends, though, followers don't have to make any effort to enjoy your content. The tweets that you write can come to them, even directly to their mobile phone if they want.

But like users and Facebook friends, followers are valuable. The more followers you have, the further your messages will reach and the more influence you'll have.

As always on the Internet, it can take time to build a large community of readers—certainly more time than most impatient publishers like to commit. But it's worth the effort and there are a number of things that you can do to reduce that time and build your list quickly.

The most important is the piece of advice that remains golden whatever you're doing on the Internet:

Produce content that's interesting, fun and valuable.

Tweets are supposed to describe what you're doing right now, but they can also include opinions, announcements, and conversations. You can write anything you want. You can even include links in your tweets to send people for further reading. Clearly, *that* can be very useful!

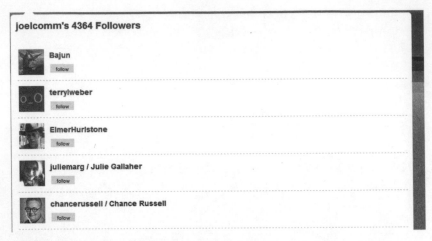

Figure 4.1   High school was a drag, but it's nice to be popular now. This is how my followers look to other followers on Twitter. Browsing follower lists is a good way to find people with updates that you want to read.

But if all you do is tell people about your new product or try to send them to some affiliate site, you'll soon find that you have no followers at all.

Don't forget that many of your followers will be receiving your tweets on their mobile phones. That means that they might be paying for them. If they don't think that they're getting value for their money—whether that's entertainment value, advice value, or any other kind of value—they'll stop following.

You might not have to pay money for followers on Twitter. But you do have to pay with good content—in 140 characters or less.

In this chapter, I'm going to explain how to build your followers. As you follow these strategies though bear in mind that the best way to create a long list of followers—*the only way to keep them reading and engaged*—is always to create great content.

Quantity or Quality: Choosing the Type of Following You Want

If you want masses and masses of followers, there's really nothing to it. It's a breeze. It's simple. It's almost foolproof.

Simply browse Twitter and follow everyone you see.

Some of those people will follow you in return automatically. Others will follow you out of manners.

Most won't follow you at all, so to get, say, 1,000 followers you might have to follow 7,000 or 8,000 Twitterers or more.

It's possible. You can do it. And if you're desperate to have a large Twitter following, it could be an interesting experiment.

But I wouldn't recommend it, and I wouldn't do that for a number of reasons.

The first is that it's going to take you a huge amount of time. It's going to be very tedious, and it's going to stuff the tweets that you see on your home page with messages from people you really don't care to follow.

In effect, you're agreeing to be spammed in return for doing some spamming yourself.

That's going to turn what should be a really fun experience into something that you're really not going to want to do for very long.

But the most important reason for not building your followers by following as many people as you possibly can is that the marketing effect will be about as strong as spam.

When you send out a tweet about your new product, your new blog post, or the release of your new e-book, only a small fraction of your followers will pay attention.

That doesn't mean that you shouldn't want a large Twitter following, though. Obviously, lots of interested followers is always going to be better than a few interested followers. But the price to be paid for having a large number of followers is often a less-targeted market and a lower conversion rate of followers to customers or users of your own site.

On the other hand, you can choose to target only those people with a direct interest in your topic; while you should be able to keep many of them active and engaged, there will be relatively few of them.

And you'll be missing other people who might be interested in what you have to say.

So what should you do? Should you attempt to build as large a following as possible? Or should you try to make it as targeted as possible?

In general, you want a core group of followers who are very interested in your topic, as many people as possible with a mild interest in your topic, and a few people who might be interested in some aspects of your topic if you get lucky.

In practice, level of interest is not easy to measure, and the chances that you'll turn a vaguely interested follower into a loyal customer will depend on your topic. If you're using your Twitter membership to drive people to a Web site and products about fantasy football, for example, you might be able to convert many people who have an interest in sports, even if they don't play fantasy football.

If you tweet about lacrosse, though, you'll probably struggle. A more focused group of followers would then be much more valuable than a large one.

One factor in deciding whether to go for as large a group as possible or focus on a select group is the broadness of your topic's appeal.

♦ If your topic is very popular—sport or cars, for example—you could do well with a large group of followers.

♦ If your topic appeals only to a small crowd—polo, for example, or solar-powered cars—then you might do better narrowing down your followers.

Note that the broadness of a topic's appeal isn't the same as the size of its niche. A marketer who had a Web site about Corvettes, for example, would be operating in a small niche. But the topic could be of interest to anyone who likes cars.

When you're considering who to target for your followers, begin with those most interested in your topic. Then expand to bring in people who might be interested in some of the topics you'll cover in your tweets.

Clearly, there's no scientific formula here.

The balance that you create between a highly targeted group of Twitter followers and a more general crowd will usually be down to a feeling that you have about your chances of bringing in people with only a slight interest in your topic.

That feeling comes from experience, and it comes from an understanding of your subject and its audience. But it is important to also understand the difference between those two types of followers and try to include both in your list of followers.

So how do you go about finding high quality followers?

Quality: How to Be Intentional about Creating Your Own Network of Experts

High quality followers can do different things. Some will be the type of followers who hang on to your every tweet, follow all your links, and buy your products.

You certainly want to have lots of those . . . but identifying them isn't easy. Few Twitterers write on their bios that they're looking to buy lots of products about Corvettes or football—or anything else.

What you can find very easily on Twitter, though, is experts.

This is really Twitter's strength. The site is stuffed with people who have great information about particular subjects and are willing to share it.

Find experts on a topic related to yours and encourage them to follow you, and you'll be giving yourself a massive and very valuable network.

The first thing you have to do, though, is find them.

Twitter has never had a very good search engine. If you were looking for a particular user on the site, you could toss their name into the search engine and hope something came up.

But that was about it.

Looking for keywords was always a huge pain and the results just weren't up to scratch.

One of the best things about Twitter, though, is that it lets developers create their own tools for the site. As we'll see later in this book, some of those tools can be very valuable. One tool was so valuable that Twitter decided to buy it. Summize's search engine is now a part of Twitter and can be reached by surfing directly to search.twitter.com or by clicking the search link at the bottom of a Twitter page.

See what's happening — *right now.*

Advanced Search

Search

Trending topics: Dixville Notch, Prop 8, Melbourne Cup, #votereport,
John McCain, Barack Obama, SNL, Hart's Location, Fallout 3, iPhone

Are you following this election? Check out Twitter E08!

Twitter Home · About Twitter Search · API · Apps · Install Search Plugin

© 2008 Twitter, Inc.

Figure 4.2 To search on Twitter, you have to get off Twitter
and use search.twitter.com.

You can enter your keywords and pull up tweets that contain
that phrase.

You'll then be able to see who's talking about your topic and,
by looking at the bios and reading their tweets, see which of those
Twitterers are the leading experts.

If you were tweeting about fantasy football, then all of the people that came back in the search results for that phrase would be
potential followers. You could try following them all and hope that
they follow you back, but that's going to take a while.

*It's much more efficient to identify the key Twitterers on the
topic and get them to follow you.*

If other people see that the expert is following you, they'll
assume that you're also an expert and want to follow you too.

Do you see how that works?

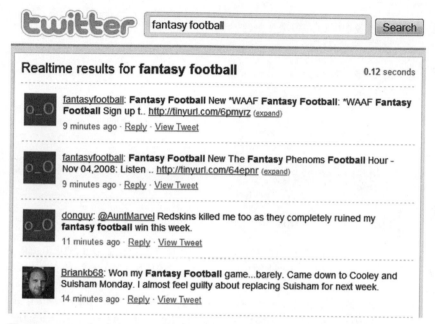

Figure 4.3 Search for "fantasy football" using Twitter's search function and you get a huge list of responses. Clue: experts usually put pictures on their profiles.

One way to succeed on Twitter is to hang out with the influence-makers. Find the top people in your topic on Twitter, and become a part of their circle.

When you're one of the prominent Twitterers on the site, you'll find it's much easier to persuade people to read your tweets. In fact, you won't have to do anything but make sure that your tweets are interesting, informative, and entertaining.

And the best news is that getting in with the expert crowd on Twitter is much easier than becoming part of the in-crowd at high school.

There are three simple steps.

1. Identify the experts.

Once you've got your list of people who have mentioned your topic in their tweets, you'll need to narrow them down to find the key influencers.

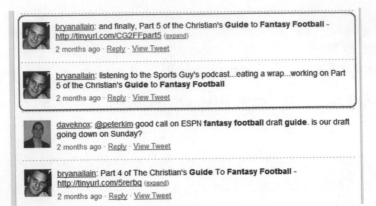

Figure 4.4   Is this one expert found?

Good signs to look out for in the search results are a picture in the profile and frequent posts. Experts understand the value of both of those things.

You can also try tweaking your search to include terms such as "guide," "guru," "expert," or "author" to help identify leaders.

When you find someone, check to see how many followers they have and when they last updated. There's no minimal number of followers a Twitterer must have to become an expert—too much depends on the topic—but if they've got four figures and post several times a day, that's a pretty good sign!

Whatever your topic, it shouldn't take you too long to produce a list of at least a dozen people who are experts to some degree in your field.

Read their tweets and follow them.

2. Gain their friendship and respect

So far, all you've done is find an expert and chosen to follow his or her updates.

That's going to be interesting, but it's not always going to turn that expert into your follower. It's only going to turn you into their follower.

And if that expert does choose to follow everyone who follows them—as many Twitterers do—that's just going to make you a face in the crowd.

To be seen as an expert yourself, you need to stand out both on the list of people they're following and on their timeline.

That happens only when you turn that Twitter connection into a friendship and a relationship cemented by respect.

Twitter provides a couple of tools to do that.

You can hit the reply icon. Or you can send them a personal message.

In general, replies are better. All of your followers will be able to see them. Even if the expert himself doesn't respond, other people will see that you're following that expert and that you have something to contribute to the discussion.

That already starts to make you look like an expert.

And if the expert responds to your reply, then you've hit the jackpot. All their followers will see that tweet and stop by to see who they're talking to. You'll pick up a ton of followers that way.

Personal messages are better if you have a special request, and you should probably only use them once you've already attracted the expert's attention through your tweets and your replies.

Otherwise, it's too much like sending a cold e-mail to someone and hoping they respond. If they don't, it's also unlikely that they'll respond to a reply, so you'll have lost the opportunity to start a conversation in public too.

However you plan to make yourself noticed, do be careful. No one is going to appreciate being bothered by everyone who follows them. Twitter might be a very friendly, open place where it's remarkably easy to exchange messages with the kind of people you'd really struggle to meet anywhere else, but if you want to build a friendship you still have to pay your dues.

3. Give back more than you take.

To do that, you have to give the expert you're hoping to add as a follower information that's truly valuable.

You can tell him something he doesn't already know.

You can point him in the direction of a resource he might find helpful.

You can even try sending him a link if it really will make a difference to what he's doing. (Links are a dime a dozen, so if you're going to reply with a link as a way of attracting attention, the content of the link has to be really good.)

And you need to hand over this valuable information as often as you can.

Twitter works because people are prepared to share valuable knowledge for free. Some of that knowledge might look worthless, but if it really is worthless, no one will follow them.

When you show anyone that you have valuable knowledge to share, you'll stand out—even to other experts.

Building up a collection of experts as followers will take a little time. Some of that time will be spent searching. Some of it will be spent reading tweets—that can be very addictive. Some of it will be spent updating your own tweets, so that you continue to be an active member of the community.

And some of it will be spent replying to other experts in your field and messaging them.

As you're doing it though, you should find that the number of followers starts to grow—first with people you respect and then with the people who respect them.

Quantity: Seven Killer Strategies to Reaching Critical Mass on Twitter

I pointed out that there are two kinds of follower lists. There are targeted follower lists made of a few people with a strong interest in your topic; and there are general follower lists made up of lots of people with a weaker interest in your topic.

I also pointed that while you'll want your list to have a mixture of both types of followers, the balance between them will depend on the nature of your topic.

We've seen that adding targeted people can be difficult. It's enjoyable and interesting. You'll learn a great deal reading the tweets of other important people on the site, but it can take time and it does depend on good tweet content and good replies.

Creating a large, general follower list can be a lot easier.

Beyond creating great content, there are a couple of important principles you need to keep.

The first is that you have to participate—*you have to become a follower*.

You can follow all sorts of people on Twitter. You can follow people you know, people you don't know and people you'd like to know.

Each time you become someone's follower, you turn up in their list, which means that they can see who's following them—and so can everyone else.

You don't have to ask their permission—all tweets are public unless the Twitterer restricts them—and you don't have to wait for them to approve you. All you have to do is hit the *Follow* button, and that person's tweets will appear on your page, and, if you want, on your mobile phone too.

Once you've found someone to follow on Twitter, you can see who they're following and who's following them. If any of those people look interesting, you can add them to your follow list—and continue.

As I mentioned, that could be all you need to do to win followers, but that would be slow going and inefficient.

The other principle you need to keep is to *join the conversation*.

So far, I've been describing Twitter as though the information flow was only one way. That isn't the case at all. While the main use of Twitter is to let other people know what you're doing, thinking, or listening to at any moment in time, the service also acts like a public, slow-motion instant messenger.

You can ask questions and provide answers to the questions other people ask.

In fact, the ability to get great answers on Twitter is one of its biggest strengths. The entire site acts like a giant forum in which experts on all sorts of subjects are willing to lend their advice to almost anyone who asks for it.

It's something that makes Twitter a very valuable resource. Every time you respond, you contribute to someone else's conversation. That makes you a valuable part of the community—and it increases the chances that other people will follow you too.

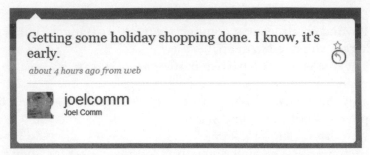

Figure 4.5 Go ahead, make my day. Tell me what you think.

Building a long list of followers doesn't happen overnight. It comes as a result of networking on the site, of providing good tweets that other people want to read, and of being active in other people's discussions.

It's the reward that comes from participating on Twitter, and best of all, it's a lot of fun to do.

But it is important. Twitter really took off once it achieved a critical mass of users—when enough people were using it that the tweets were interesting to read and there was a good chance that you could find someone you wanted to follow.

Critical mass is important to your follower list, too. You need to have enough followers to enable your tweets to spark a conversation.

You need to have enough followers to be able to convert at least some of them to customers, users, or clients.

And you need to have enough followers to spread word of your tweets and inspire other Twitterers to tell their friends about you.

Although there aren't any foolproof shortcuts to creating your list, there a few things that you can do to cut the time and build your list faster. Here are seven different ways to do it:

1. Look for people you already know.

Let's start with the very easiest method: Look for people you already know.

Twitter is popular enough now that there is a good chance that at least some of the people in your address book are already Twittering away.

As we've seen, Twitter lets you find those people on the site by taking a leaf out of Facebook's page. It can scan your Web mail and compare your contacts to the people in its own database.

Initially, I recommended that you do *not* do this. I believe that it's a better idea to wait until your profile has been created and you've started posting tweets.

Once you've done that though, you're free to go. Just hit the "Find People" link at the top of the page, enter your e-mail address and password, and let Twitter do the searching. The site will then return a list of all the people in your contact book who are using Twitter. Follow them, reply to some of their tweets or send them a personal message to make sure that they see you're following them, and there's a good chance they'll follow you too.

That's the good news.

The bad news is that this only works for Web-based mail. At the moment, there is no simple way to search your Outlook contacts for Twitterers.

So you'll have to cheat.

Open a free Web-based e-mail account such as Gmail or Yahoo! Mail, if you don't have one already. Then export your contact list from Outlook and import it into your new account. Your new mail service will explain how to do it, but it shouldn't take more than a few minutes.

You won't have to actually use that account, but you will now be able to search your contacts automatically on Twitter to see if any of them are Twittering.

How many followers will this method give you?

It depends on the size of your contact list and the chances that a large part of it will be on the site. You're unlikely to pick up thousands of followers right away, but there is a good chance that you'll be able to add a few new readers, and there's an even better chance that those people will follow you in return.

2. Tweet your blog.

One of the most common goals of a good Twitter presence will often be to direct followers to your Web site.

Once they reach your site, your followers will be able to read posts that are longer than 140 characters. They'll be able to click on your ads, and they'll be able to buy your products.

They won't be able to do any of those things on your Twitter page.

But another of your aims will also be to build a closer connection with the users you have, so that you become a part of their lives. That means your users will return to your site more often and they'll be more likely to take you up on your special offers.

Those users, then, are a valuable pool of potential followers.

If you can show your users your tweets and bring them onto your Twitter page, you'll be able to massively increase the number of your followers.

And Twitter makes it very easy to post tweets on a Web site.

Figure 4.6   Joe Teh puts his tweets on his blog, techielobang.com/blog.

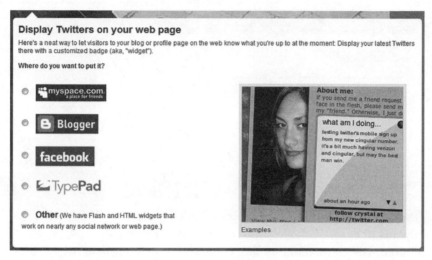

Figure 4.7 Twitter's own widgets make publicizing your tweets as simple as click, cut, and paste.

Surf to twitter.com/badges and select the kind of page on which you'd like to put your tweets. The site offers MySpace, Facebook, Blogger and Typepad as automatic options, but also provides widgets that work just about everywhere.

Once you've chosen the type of badge you want, you'll be able to customize it and copy the code. Insert the code where you want the page to appear on your site, then upload and check to see it's all looking the way it should.

As always, it's a good idea to make the customization match the design of your site as closely as possible. You want your tweets to look like they're part of your site, so that readers see it as extra content, not something that's been brought in from outside—like an ad.

The result should be that you'll have some extra content on your site, your users will be able to see your tweets on your page and they'll be tempted to click through to your Twitter page to see all the tweets they missed.

If you're getting thousands of users to your Web site every week and only a small fraction of them actually follow you on Twitter, you can still end up with a massive number of followers using this method.

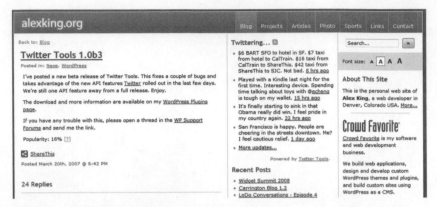

Figure 4.8   Alex King uses Twitter Tools on his own Web site. Note how his updates look like content to make sure they're read, not ignored. The More updates link leads to his Twitter page, where his users can follow him.

For WordPress users though, the news doesn't look quite so good.

In fact, it's even better.

You'll probably have noticed that WordPress isn't listed as one of the badges that Twitter offers. While you can select "other," a better option is to use the Twitter Tools plugin. You can download it for free from alexking.org/projects/wordpress.

This plugin won't just show your tweets on your site, it will also let you send tweets from your blog, turn your posts into tweets, and issue alerts, complete with a link, whenever you write a new blog post. (Alex, a Web developer in Denver, Colorado, has a bunch of other very cool WordPress plugins and themes that you can check out on his site, too.)

3. Pay your followers!

This might not sound like the smartest—or the cheapest—way to bring in large numbers of followers...but you could just consider paying people to follow you.

Giving away freebies is a marketing standard. You create goodwill, let potential customers try your products before they buy, and build a list of clients that you can draw on in the future.

As long as you follow the simple rule that what you give away should cost you little but have high value to the recipient, you should find that offering freebies can have a fantastic effect on your revenues.

I've given away hundreds of thousands of dollars' worth of goods through my Web sites and seminars—and I've received many times that in return.

The principle can work in exactly the same way on Twitter to incentivize Twitterers to follow you.

Angie Jones (twitter.com/fitbizwoman), who produces a subscription-based fitness newsletter, for example, uses her Twitter bio to promise a free recipe e-book to anyone who follows her.

E-mailing that recipe book will cost her nothing. In fact, when she asks her new follower for an address, she'll be building up an e-mail list of people interested in exactly the sort of information she offers.

Giving away that recipe book actually pays her by giving her something more valuable in return: a targeted list.

It also shows her followers what she can do and what her customers will receive—and it gives people a great reason to follow her tweets.

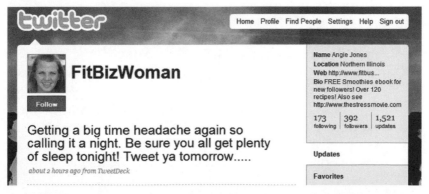

Figure 4.9 Angie Jones's bio promises a freebie to followers. But is it clear what Angie does on this page? She might be better off using the bio to explain that she's a fitness coach and offering the freebie in a sidebar.

http://buy-tees.net is the first international tshirt blog to ask for their customised springleap coupon code to give to their readers. *7:41 PM Oct 16th from web*

http://www.imod.co.za is the first blog to display their customised springleap coupon code. Don't wait till your coupon code name is taken! *7:27 PM Oct 16th from web*

remember that the springleap 40% OFF Sale is now ending at 10am TODAY. Use coupon code G71RB84 for FORTY PERCENT DISCOUNT on everything! *3:01 AM Oct 13th from web*

like our profile image? it's the featured designer for september - the amazingly talented Colwyn with "Tiger Hug" *8:53 PM Oct 12th from web*

the 40% off Sale on springleap.com has been extended to 10am Monday morning (South African time) - DON'T MISS OUT ON THIS ONE *8:46 PM Oct 12th from web*

@nickjackson we did send you an email replying to yours. did you get it? *3:59 PM Oct 12th from web in reply to nickjackson*

Figure 4.10 SpringLeap pays its followers to keep in touch—and generates sales, too.

SpringLeap (twitter.com/springleap), a South African designer t-shirt company, takes a slightly different approach. Rather than rewarding Twitterers immediately when they follow their tweets, SpringLeap offers constant rewards in the form of time-limited discount codes in its tweets.

For anyone interested in SpringLeap's unique t-shirts, following the company's tweets pays. And the company gets to make sure that people read its company news, are aware of new designs and revisit to shop often.

4. **Respond to requests.**

One topic that I'm going to keep coming back to in this book is that successful Twitterers use Twitter to do more than make announcements.

They use it to spark conversations. And they use it to *join* conversations.

Those conversations are open and public, but that just means that they're even more valuable. When anyone can see who's saying what in a Twitter exchange, anyone can follow the links back to the Twitterers who impress them and follow them as well.

Sometimes that might just mean hitting the reply button and coming up with a good response. Often though, other Twitterers offer golden opportunities to jump into a chat by asking a question.

Provide a good answer, and you get to look like a bigger expert than the original Twitterer.

There are a couple of rules to follow here though.

The first is that any information you provide has to be genuinely good. Saying, "Yeah, I'm having trouble with that too . . ." or quoting from Wikipedia is not going to do you any good.

People will follow your tweets only if they feel that you have information that's worth reading. That's one reason that it's a good idea to answer questions about your subject rather than any question that you happen to see.

You'll pick up people with an interest in your topic, but you'll also get a bigger opportunity to show off your expertise.

Not sure @don_draper goes to work today. Strange, but he owes us. Maybe we should all do something when Sally gets back from school. *10:54 AM Oct 27th from web*

@JodiJe Simply had plenty of practice advising Don on these issues. *10:52 AM Oct 27th from web in reply to JodiJe*

@dossy What does that mean, Eliza-style? *10:51 AM Oct 27th from web in reply to dossy*

@andlj1967 Thank you for being next to me. It'll take both of us a while for that news to sink in... *10:50 AM Oct 27th from web in reply to andlj1967*

@mikepratt Rather: was it something I said that kept you from returning my gesture initially? *10:49 AM Oct 27th from web in reply to mikepratt*

@trench Sorry, drop what? *10:49 AM Oct 27th from web in reply to trench*

@danperry I was hoping we become friends. It seems you opted not to. *10:48 AM Oct 27th from web in reply to danperry*

@dustindk Thank you. Somehow, he didn't seem more excited that me, though. *10:47 AM Oct 27th from web in reply to DustinDK*

Figure 4.11 Betty Draper (twitter.com/betty_draper) is a character on the AMC show *Mad Men*. She also tweets—or, rather, a fan does it on her behalf—and has more than 4,300 followers. Reply to her tweets or answer your questions, and when she comments back, you'll be putting your name in front of thousands of people. Who else can you find with a large following?

The second rule is that the more popular the questioner, the greater the benefits of lending them a hand—or even providing them with a good reply.

When they thank you or comment back, lots of people will see their response, wonder who you are and stop by your Twitter page to find out.

This is a strategy followed by Dan Perry (twitter.com/danperry), a search engine optimization expert at Cars.com, and he already has more than 850 followers.

5. Mobilize your social network.

Here's one I really like! Twitter is extremely powerful, but it becomes even more powerful when it's used as one part of a marketing strategy that uses different elements of social media.

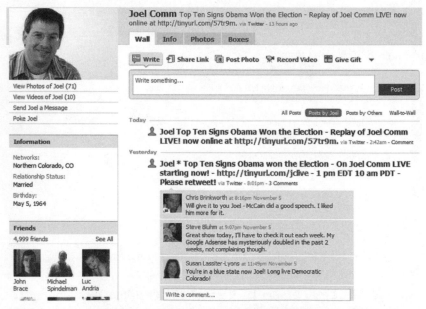

Figure 4.12 My Facebook page is stuffed with Twitter content. With 5,000 people to bring to my Twitter timeline, why not? And check out how those tweets spark conversations here. On Facebook, tweets turn followers and friends into a community.

Because each social media site offers different features and works in a different way, by making them all work together you make sure that you're sharing the audience between each site.

Facebook, for example, gives me much more flexibility than Twitter. It lets me post photos, run groups, and interact with my friends in all sorts of different ways. I have 5,000 friends on Facebook—the maximum the site allows. By placing my tweets on Facebook too, I'm able to show all of those 5,000 people my Twitter content and give them a reason to follow me there as well. They'll want to make sure that they're not missing anything.

And this can work the other way too. If you see someone on MySpace or Facebook with lots of friends and who tweets as well, follow them on Twitter and comment on their Facebook Wall. There's a good chance that they'll follow you back, and their friends and followers will want to check you out as well.

6. **Put your Twitter name in your signatures.**

Such an easy thing to do, such an old idea...and so often forgotten.

As soon as a new technology comes along, there can be a tendency to forget about all the old standards, like the value of including your URL on your business card and on your e-mail and forum signatures.

Just as that strategy can drive plenty of interested people to your Web site, adding your Twitter URL to those signatures can have exactly the same effect.

Twitter might let you search your contact list for people who are already Twittering, and it might let you send those who aren't on the site an invitation to join up, but if all you want to do is alert people on your e-mail list—in forums, and anyone else you chat with online—that you're Twittering, then this is a very simple way to do it.

7. **Run a contest.**

I pointed out that one way to build up followers is to reward them for following you. We saw that one way that

Twitterers are doing that is to give them a freebie as soon as they hit the *Follow* button.

Another way is to include discount codes in the tweets to keep people reading.

Jason Cormier (twitter.com/jasoncormier), who runs a search marketing and social media agency, takes a very different approach for his clients. He helps them to organize contests on Twitter.

SmartyPig, for example, a kind of online savings bank, asks a question on Twitter at a specific time. Followers have 15 minutes to reply. Three winners are then selected at random from those who sent in the correct answer and receive a $100 gift card.

Go! Good Luck tweeps! *5:00 PM Oct 30th from web*

SmartyPig is expanding into what country next month? *5:00 PM Oct 30th from web*

Okay - it's 3pm CST - here's the $100 question: *5:00 PM Oct 30th from web*

Almost ready out there? About 2 minutes until the big $100 questions comes out! *4:57 PM Oct 30th from web*

5. We'll choose the winners - and post the video of it all on our blog - we'll tweet as soon as it's up! *4:52 PM Oct 30th from web*

4. We use a random number generator and pick 20 names out of the pool of correct answers. *4:52 PM Oct 30th from web*

3. We will let you know when the 15 minutes has expired and the contest has closed. *4:51 PM Oct 30th from web*

2. reply @smartypig with your answer - we don't even look at DM's during the contest. *4:51 PM Oct 30th from web*

1. We will ask a question and you will have 15 minutes to respond. *4:50 PM Oct 30th from web*

Alright, 10 minutes to go - if you don't already know the drill, here it is: *4:50 PM Oct 30th from web*

Just over 15 minutes until the contest! Get ready, tweeps! *4:42 PM Oct 30th from web*

Figure 4.13   SmartyPig (twitter.com/smartypig) runs contests on Twitter to keep its followers reading and make sure that all of its customers follow its tweets.

One contest generated almost 100 correct answers in the space of fifteen minutes.

The big advantage of a competition like this is that it's happening in real time. The company could just as easily have asked the question on its blog and said that it would be announcing the winners a week later.

By running the contest live, through Twitter, it collects all of its customers together in one place at one time, turns them into a community and creates a party atmosphere too.

And, of course, it also makes sure that all of its customers are following its tweets.

Twitterank and Page Rank

There are all sorts of different strategies that you can use to build up your follower list. But the number next to your follower list is just one measure of success on Twitter.

No less important—and perhaps even more important—is the extent to which you're the focus of conversation.

Because Twitter is like a giant open chat, the more people who reply to your tweets, the more influential your posts. It's a great sign that people are interested in what you have to say and want to take part in the discussion.

That's the theory, at least, behind Twitterank (twitterank.com), a service that uses the number of incoming replies to give each Twitterer a score that supposed to represent their popularity. The theory is similar to Google's page rank, which rates the importance of Web sites based, among other things, on the number and quality of incoming links the site receives.

Twitterank lets you see your own score, and you can toss in the usernames of other Twitterers to see their scores, too.

Twitterank was created by programmer Ryo Chijiiwa, and it caused a bit of a storm when it first came out. Because Ryo asked for usernames and passwords, a rumor spread that he was hoarding personal data and that the service was a giant phishing scam. That appears not to be true—Ryo has since made clear that all passwords are automatically deleted as soon as the Twitterank has been calculated—but it was a pretty good example of the speed joelcomm's **twitterrank is:**

199.66

approx. 99.77 percentile
(23.13% confidence) wtf?

URL: http://twitterank.com/view/joelcomm
Get your twitterank!

Figure 4.14 According to Twitterank, I'm pretty popular ... maybe.

with which information (and a good idea) can spread across the Twitterverse.

The real question, of course, is how useful this stuff is. The service was created as a bit of fun. Unlike Google's page rank, Twitterank isn't going to affect where you turn up in search results or how much traffic you're likely to receive.

It certainly won't affect the amount of money you receive in advertising revenues.

However, you might consider it one way to measure how well you're managing to motivate discussions in comparison to other Twitterers. You can also take a look at the list of the top 50 Twitterers to see what they're doing to get those replies. For many, it seems to consist of being a well-known mover and shaker off Twitter as much as the type of tweets they're posting.

Interestingly though, tweets also receive page ranks.

Paste a tweet into Google and you'll find that it's been indexed in the search engine.

My suspicion is that this works the same as any Web page. Since I have links going to my Twitter page from other authority sites, Google raises the page rank of my Twitter page and the value of

Twitter / Joel Comm: **Barnes & Noble book** signin ... ⊼ ⊠
Barnes & Noble book signing was fun @successcoach. I guess I need to blog about it.
about 1 hour ago from web. Joel-look2_bigger · joelcomm. Joel Comm.
twitter.com/joelcomm/status/1018727961 - 9k - Cached - Similar pages - ⊚

    Twitter / joelcomm ⊼ ⊠
    Barnes & Noble book signing was fun @successcoach. I guess I need to blog about it.
    ... @successcoach Magpie works technically, but they **need** advertisers. ...
    twitter.com/joelcomm - 41k - Cached - Similar pages - ⊚
    More results from twitter.com »

Twitter / joelcomm ⊼ ⊠
Barnes & Noble book signing was fun @successcoach. I guess I need to blog about it.
about 13 hours ago from web. @successcoach Magpie works technically, ...
https://explore.twitter.com/joelcomm - 41k - Cached - Similar pages - ⊚

Figure 4.15　Hey look, I'm on Google too.

my outgoing links. Whether that's worth anything to me is hard to say. I can't imagine that anyone's going to look for a tweet from me on Google, and trying to target keywords so that your Twitter page will turn up at the top of search rankings is unlikely to be worth the effort.

But it is an interesting quirk of Twitter.

Creating a long list of followers is always going to be one of the most important tasks that you do on Twitter. It's a challenge that requires first deciding what kind of followers you want: an audience that's niched and mostly targeted; one that's large but general; or a balanced combination of the two.

It will then involve a great deal of following and reading. You'll have to reply to tweets that other people have posted, place tweets of your own and track down the people you know—and would like to know—on the site.

It's a process that takes time. While there are strategies to make that process faster—and I discussed several of them in this chapter—no one ever builds a four-figure follower list overnight.

That's because above all, creating a large following on Twitter requires writing good tweets—the kind that people actually want to read and that make them feel that you're going to have more good information for them in the future.

That's what I discuss in the next chapter.

5

The Art of the Tweet

The moment it became clear that the Internet could be a good way for businesses to make money, one simple rule stood out:

Sites with good content succeeded; sites with poor content failed.

That didn't mean that lots of people didn't try earning money with poor content. They did. They still do.

And they still fail.

Sure, a Web site owner can find a wordsmith in Mumbai to churn out articles for $5 each so that he can have somewhere to put his ads, but even at those low rates, he's still going to lose money.

If the content isn't good, no one will want to read it.

Instead of putting effort into creating good articles, the publisher will have to put even more effort into dragging people to his Web pages.

And he'll have to keep doing it, because once a user has visited a poor site once, he won't come back.

That rule holds true on Twitter, too.

To build followers and keep them engaged, you have to produce good content.

The only difference is in the nature of good content on Twitter.

Because you only have 140 characters, you can't create the long list posts that are so popular in social media sites. You can't create in-depth how-to articles that give people valuable knowledge and help them to complete important tasks. And any interviews you wanted to run would have to consist of very short questions and one-word answers.

Good content on Twitter needs to be entertaining. It needs to be informative. It needs to be valuable.

And it needs to be short.

In this chapter, I'm going to look at some of the ways to produce great Twitter content, the kind of tweets that build followers, keep your readers coming back for more, and engage them in your conversation.

I'm going to start though by talking about the rules.

Tweet Etiquette

Every conversation has rules. We know not to interrupt someone when they're talking. We know not to use bad language when we talk. We know not to talk too loudly.

And we know too how and when to break all of the rules.

Exactly the same is true for a Twitter conversation.

The site hasn't been around for long, but Twitterers have already tried to figure out something like a Twittering etiquette.

Some of those etiquette rules are smart, sensible, and should always be followed. Others are smart, sensible, and should usually be followed.

While it's important to know the rules, it's just as important then to know when to break them—and what happens when you do.

1. **Don't spam.**

This is one rule you can't break. Spammers don't survive long on Twitter. They don't build followers. Any followers they do get don't read their tweets and the number of conversions they can generate will be so tiny that as a marketing method, you'd probably be better off printing a thousand flyers, folding them into paper airplanes and tossing them out of your office window.

There are all sorts of different ways to spam on Twitter.

As we've seen, one way is to follow lots and lots of people in the hope that some of them follow you in return. That's not just ineffective, it also turns up clearly in your bio.

Whenever someone's bio shows that they're follow-ing several thousand people but only being followed by a handful, that's a pretty good sign that they're looking to spam. They're trying to build up followers who will follow them out of politeness rather than because they have interesting content.

Twitterers often steer clear of people like that.

The spamming itself though is done by constantly send-ing out tweets that say things like: "I've just put up a new blog post—check it out!" or "Sign up for my RSS feed!"

You can send out tweets like this occasionally. But as we'll see later in this section, they have to be mixed in with other tweets too. Otherwise, you're just spamming, and that's annoying.

Worse, it doesn't work.

2. Follow style rules.

Twitter's founders may have had mobile phones in mind when they designed the service, and plenty of users may be typing their updates from their handheld devices, but Twitter isn't exactly the same as SMS messaging.

That means the language needs to look more like real words than the usual SMS-style abbreviations.

It goes without saying that typing in uppercase letters looks like you're shouting, but in addition to avoiding all uppercase, you should spell out words completely and avoid using numbers instead of letters whenever possible. (For example, "late" is not spelled "l8" and "to" is two letters, not one number.)

That might mean more typing, but the reasoning is sensi-ble. "Heading 2 town l8. Dont no wot 4" is hard for the reader to understand. It's only good manners—and good marketing sense—for you to put in the work so that your readers don't have to.

There are exceptions, of course. If you're really strapped for space, this is a rule you can break, but understand that you're forcing your followers to make an effort.

What is permissible, though, is to use symbols such as @ and = and to skip some of the grammar. The question Twitter

---

Apologies to those who don't like me using abbreviations and numbers "4" words but constraints of Twitter sometimes enforce such .... x *3:50 PM Oct 27th from web*

@MelanieSchicker To twitter means to chatter like a bird "and gathering swallows twitter in the skies" J. Keats ... often used of gossip! x *3:46 PM Oct 27th from web in reply to MelanieSchicker*

@breenster "why do you twitter?" Gosh,why do you? I like 2 tweet while travelling the world,I like following & being followed,I like the new *1:24 PM Oct 27th from web in reply to breenster*

Figure 5.1 Stephen Fry apologizes for his lack of style.

asks might be "What are you doing now?" but you don't have to begin your answer by saying "I am..."

Sentence fragments such "About to start watching the football. Can't wait." are fine.

3. **Give credit for retweets.**

One of the things that makes Twitter such a powerful tool is the fact that information placed on the site can quickly go viral. When one person spots a good tweet, they can pass that message on to their own followers,and soon it's spreading right across the Twitterverse and beyond.

For a marketer, that's like hitting the jackpot.

On Twitter, it's done by retweeting.

Twitterers can simply copy someone else's tweet and tweet it themselves...but they must give credit to the original Twitterer. The format for retweets, then, looks like this:

"Retweet @username: original tweet."

So if you wanted to retweet this post from my timeline:

"Spontaneous LIVE broadcast! join me now with special guest! http://tinyurl.com/jclive"

then you would tweet:

"Retweet @joelcomm: Spontaneous LIVE broadcast! join me now with special guest! http://tinyurl.com/jclive"

Any comments you want to add to the retweet can go at the beginning or in brackets at the end:

"Not missing this! Retweet @joelcomm: Spontaneous LIVE broadcast! join me now with special guest! http://tinyurl.com/jclive"

Figure 5.2   Dave Baldwin (twitter.com/highonbeing
dave) shares the love—and a tweet.

"Retweet @joelcomm: Spontaneous LIVE broadcast!
join me now with special guest! http://tinyurl.com/
jclive (Not missing this!)"

The etiquette is simple enough. Sharing tweets is easy
to understand, too. It might not be original content, but if
your followers would find the original tweet interesting, why
shouldn't you share it?

The tricky bit is to get other people to retweet for you.
While you can ask specifically for retweets—and some people do—it's not really good form.

If your tweets are interesting enough, people will share
them with their friends and followers—and those friends and
followers will come to your page to find out who you are.

4. **Stick to 140 characters.**

You *have* to stick to 140 characters, right? That's all they
give you, and they do it for a good reason. Being starved of
space stops you waffling and sparks your creativity. It's what
Twitter is all about.

Well, yes and no.

Twitter gives you 140 characters because that's all that
can fit through SMS systems. If mobile phone companies

could handle messages of 200 characters, then that's probably how long our tweets would be.

Even though the limit is fairly arbitrary, it does make sense to keep to it as much as possible.

The alternative is to show half-complete tweets and offer links for people to continue reading or break messages up so that they're sent over several tweets.

You can see this happening sometimes on Twitter, and it rarely looks good. Readers expect the content on Twitter to be small. They expect to be able to read and absorb it in one bite. These are content snacks, not three-course meals with coffee.

Writing a thought that takes more than 140 characters and spreading it over three or four tweets is giving people more than they want. It also makes you look like you're dominating the conversation.

Chat with a friend, and you'll take turns speaking. You'll speak, your friend will respond, and then you'll continue. Keep talking without giving your friend a chance to offer his response and you'll start to sound rude.

Multiple tweets can have the same effect upon Twitter.

Again, this doesn't mean you should *never* break up a long tweet. And it certainly doesn't mean that you shouldn't post one tweet after another.

Later, after playing tourist, we'll meet at @web2asia 's offices to see a bunch of cool startups. The #china20 tour... http://ff.im/eg6 *12:11 AM yesterday from FriendFeed*

Back in Shanghai, about to go play tourist with @christinelu and @rocmanusa. Damn the pollution here is extreme. My... http://ff.im/ef6 *12:09 AM yesterday from FriendFeed*

Video of Seagate hard drives being tested: http://www.viddler.com/expl... more video coming in... http://ff.im/aGE *4:41 PM Nov 7th from FriendFeed*

Figure 5.3 Tech expert and super-blogger Robert Scoble (twitter.com/scobleizer) wrote some of the rules for tweeting and says that they should be broken. Here, he turns his tweets into teasers for FriendFeed, a service that links together social media sites.

What it does mean is that you should be aware of the effect you can create in your timeline when you do either.

5. Follow people who follow you.

How many people you should follow on Twitter can always make for a great discussion point. Follow thousands of people and you're not going to be able to read all of their tweets. Inevitably, you'll miss tweets you'd really like to read, and you'll look like someone who has lots of acquaintances but no real friends.

In practice, it doesn't always work this way. I follow more than 1,700 people. That's a lot less than the 4,500 or so who follow me, and while I know I'm missing tweets, I love the fact that when I look at my Twitter page I can see a huge variety of different conversations taking place.

It's a bit like strolling through the lobby during a break at a conference. I can choose which conversations to join and which to walk past. I find it very valuable, but I also don't want to overdo it so I don't follow everyone who follows me.

That makes me a feel a little rude, but I do feel that I have to control the number of tweets that pass across my home page and keep them focused on conversations that relate to Internet marketing.

You might feel different.

You might want—at least at the beginning—to reward everyone who follows you by following them in return. There are plenty of top Twitterers who do this.

Similarly, you might prefer only to follow close friends and people you already know. That will make you look anti-social and cliquey, which is not the best image for a marketer, but it's possible.

Ultimately, I think this is one place where eventually you have to skip the etiquette and do what works. As your follower list grows, you'll have to start being a little bit choosier about who you follow in return—and your followers will just have to understand that you're being selective, not rude.

Spend any time on Twitter and you're going to come across plenty of other rules too. Some purists, for example, argue that your tweets should only describe what you're doing, not what you're thinking or planning to do. I think that's far too restrictive: if it sparks a conversation and entertains your followers, it's a fair topic. If they don't like it, they should read someone else's tweets.

And that's really the ultimate test of tweet etiquette: how other people react and how you would react to the same kind of thing.

If you're building followers and they're responding to what you're writing, you're following the right rules.

The Benefits of Following Before Twittering

One of the results of flexible Twitter etiquette is that it's inevitable that every Twitterer ends up making and following their own rules.

Some follow everyone who follows them; others don't.

Some reply to everyone who replies to them; others don't reply to anyone.

Some ask questions and expect followers to answer; others never do.

That means before you dive into a conversation—and even before you get your own tweeting career fully under way with regular tweets that market your products and your services—it's important to spend time following others and reading their tweets.

Clearly that's going to take a little time, but the advantages are important.

First, you'll get to see the etiquette rules that others are following. If you can see that someone you'd like to add as a follower has 1,000 followers but only follows 40 people, you shouldn't be too upset if he doesn't add you the minute you add him.

You'll also see whether he thinks using numbers instead of letters is annoying or acceptable (based on whether he does it himself) and what he likes to tweet about.

No less importantly, you'll be able to see who's following him so that you can follow them too and understand who might follow you if you turn this Twitterer into a follower.

But perhaps most crucially, if you spend time following and reading tweets before you dive into a conversation you'll be able to see what caused the Twitterer to respond to one of his followers.

This is what you want to happen when you tweet directly to a Twitterer by hitting the "reply" button. Your name and a link

joelcomm

> ✓ Following

@Christinahills wait till we release
TextCastLive.com - gonna be earthshaking
in the marketing world!

about 3 hours ago from web in reply to christinahills

Figure 5.4   What did Christina Hills (twitter.com/christinahills) say to get her name and link in front of more than 4,700 people?

to your Twitter page appear in their timeline. All of their followers can see it and will want to know who you are.

It's fantastic marketing.

By looking at the questions that other repliers asked and the responses they posted, you'll be able to understand what you have to reply—or post—to win that prize.

How to Join a Conversation

One of the things that makes Twitter so appealing is that it's such an open community. There might be several million people on the site talking about what they're doing and chatting with other Twitterers, but you really do feel that every one of them could be your friend if you wanted them to be.

That's a remarkable feeling, and it's something you can't find on many social media sites. Facebook, for example, requires a potential friend to confirm that he or she knows you before you can even see their profile, let alone add them as a contact.

Twitter is much more communal. Everyone on the site seems to be available to provide information, swap a tip, or hand over some valuable piece of advice. There's only one condition . . .

. . . you must give them something valuable in return.

That means when you want to take part in a conversation that you can see happening on Twitter on a topic that looks interesting, you can't simply introduce yourself and expect to be welcomed.

Twitter might feel like a giant networking room, but it doesn't work in the same way.

If other people on the site want to know who you are, they can stop by your profile, read your bio, and surf through to your Web site.

What they really want to know is what you have to contribute to the debate. And that can't be a plug for you.

Or rather, it can't *just* be a plug for you.

If all you do is say something like "I covered this topic in my blog! Check it out here: http://tinyurl.com/sdsdsf" then you're going to sound like a salesman.

If, on the other hand, you provide one solid piece of information that you drew out of that post *and* provide a link to a place where readers can learn more, then you're paying for the return reply.

Do you see the difference?

The first type of tweet is an ad; the second type is a contribution to the conversation.

But you don't have to do anything as blatant as including a link in your tweet to get the benefits of joining a conversation if you do it right.

Christina Hills (twitter.com/christinahills), for example, is an entrepreneur who helps other business owners with their marketing. Because of her expertise with one particular shopping cart system, she is known as "The Shopping Cart Queen." I know that many of her followers would be interested in the sort of information that I provide in my timeline, and I'm sure that she recognizes that some of my followers would find her strategies helpful too.

By joining each other's conversations we each get to learn new things and we expose our followers to the others' expertise.

It's a technique that can only work through conversation.

That's just one way to join a conversation, and as you can see, it's incredibly simple. In fact, you can think of it as a little like a traditional link exchange. The better your tweets and the more popular your Twitter page, the easier it's going to be to get your name on other people's timeline.

christinahills

Follow

Having fun playing around with the Amazon Associate program and add book links to website. This is a great tool for non techie authors!

about 5 hours ago from web

@joelcomm yeah the iPhone is making me rethink my whole marketing. Mobile is the way to go! *about 16 hours ago from TwitterFon in reply to joelcomm*

Saturday morn: soccer field is wet. Almost last game of the season. Maggie is playing defense and looking tired *about 16 hours ago from TwitterFon*

Getting ready to send a replay broadcast, and prep for my webinar today in less than 1 hour. *2:16 PM Nov 7th from web*

This iPhone is making me want to convert to a Mac. I love the UI and MobileMe *3:36 AM Nov 7th from TwitterFon*

Figure 5.5 Joining a conversation on Twitter. Christina Hills had written a tweet about the iPhone. I replied with my own contribution to the discussion, and she responded. We get to talk about the iPhone, and our followers get to follow a quick chat between two marketing coaches about a tool we're both using.

@DanNickerson is now known as "NickerMan" *6:14 PM Nov 7th from web in reply to dannickerson*

Hanging out with rock star, Robert Lee Molton - http://www.rockguitarlicks.... *4:20 PM Nov 7th from web*

@christinahills the iphone is the first phone that knows how I want to use it. Very impressive. *3:37 AM Nov 7th from web in reply to christinahills*

Winner of the "Click Here to Order" contest is visiting us in Loveland today. Bright guy! *4:30 PM Nov 6th from web*

Figure 5.6 My reply to Christina's tweet. I add my opinion . . . and we're talking!

@problogger Good deal. Having such a huge reputation has its value. *8:10 AM yesterday from tukirl in reply to problogger*

@problogger How did you secure those Twitter accounts? How to go about it? Through $$$? *8:05 AM yesterday from tukirl in reply to problogger*

@Spartz I secured the twitter usernames with a trade - some of my time for the names *8:07 AM yesterday from TweetDeck in reply to Spartz*

Figure 5.7 Professional blogger Darren Rowse keeps his community close by answering their questions. Here, he answers Spartz's (twitter.com/spartz) question about his acquisition of a Twitter username for his new Twitter blog Twitip (www.twitip.com).

Providing information isn't the only way to join a conversation though. An alternative method is to ask for information.

This is another good reason to read someone's timeline before you join the conversation. Some Twitterers are fantastic at answering people's questions. Others aren't so hot. That might be because they don't have the time. It could be because they have too many followers. Or it might just be because that's not what they want to do with their Twitter membership.

Read the old tweets first, and you'll be able to see how often the Twitterer answers—and what kind of questions they're likely to answer, too.

How to Be Interesting on Twitter

This is what it all comes down to. You can follow etiquette, offer great tips in replies to other people's tweets, and ask questions that get your name in the timelines of the most important Twitterers on Twitter.

But none of that will mean a thing if you don't have the sort of content on your own timeline that will turn those visitors into followers—and your followers into customers, clients, or regular users.

Even though Twitter asks a very specific question, there's a huge range of different kinds of content that you can write as tweets. In this section, I'm going to describe the most important and the most effective kinds of tweets.

In general, you can divide your tweets into two types: *broadcasts* and *conversations*.

It should be clear now that Twitter can be used in two ways. One way is to convey information—to tell your followers what you're doing, thinking, or have been doing until now.

That's a one-way stream. Tweets like these don't expect replies. They're meant to be informative and entertaining, and while people might reply to them, their first function is to enable the Twitterer to tell his followers something they don't know.

It's little different from the way that a television station works.

The second types of tweets are those that are intended to spark discussions, or which form a part of a discussion. Questions and answers to other people's questions and replies are obviously conversation tweets, but they can be much more subtle than that. Just tweeting something controversial or even just writing the sort of thing that people will want to know more about can make for a good conversation tweet too.

And having a conversation brings all sorts of benefits.

We've seen that when someone replies to one of your tweets, your name and link appear on their timeline, winning you more followers. Each discussion starter then can act like a viral ad.

You can reply to their replies, giving you easy additional content and an enjoyable conversation.

And the discussion as a whole can help to build a community and bring your followers—and potential customers—closer to your brand.

Ideally, a Twitter timeline should contain a good mixture of both kinds of tweets. If you're busy replying and chatting to your followers, you might start to look a little too cliquey. You'll probably find that you'll be talking to the same group of people and, worse, that you won't have complete control over the conversation. Instead of saying what you want to say, you'll feel obligated to discuss the topics that your followers want to ask you about.

If that's what you want your timeline to do, that's fine. Lots of people use Twitter in that way—much like a large, open instant messaging board—but if you're using Twitter for marketing, you will need to keep control of the message and the subjects of the discussions.

On the other hand, if all you do is broadcast, then your timeline is going to look a little dull. Although there are some very successful Twitterers who do nothing but broadcast—President Obama's campaign tweeting picked up almost 125,000 followers, but did little more than tell people which rallies the candidate was addressing—most Twitterers find it pays to combine the two approaches.

Use broadcast tweets to make sure the information you want to share gets across.

And use conversation tweets to turn those followers into a community, keep them coming back and make sure that the issues they want discussed are addressed.

Here are some of the most effective kinds of tweets that you can send:

LINK TWEETS: "THIS IS WHAT I'M WORKING ON NOW."

This is probably the most common type of broadcast tweet, if only because there are a number of Twitter apps that let bloggers turn their posts into tweets automatically.

It's also very useful.

If you've put up a new blog post, then you'll want people to know about it and read it, and many of your followers will want to do just that. Darren Rowse, for example, has a second Twitter account at twitter.com/digitalps to promote his digital photography Web site, Digital Photography School (digital-photography-school.com/blog/).

Even thought this timeline does nothing but announce automatically new posts that have been published on Darren's photography blog, it has almost 1,200 followers . . . *and generates more than 100 visits from each tweet.*

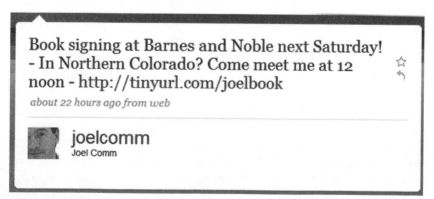

Book signing at Barnes and Noble next Saturday! - In Northern Colorado? Come meet me at 12 noon - http://tinyurl.com/joelbook

about 22 hours ago from web

joelcomm
Joel Comm

Figure 5.8   Read all about it here . . .

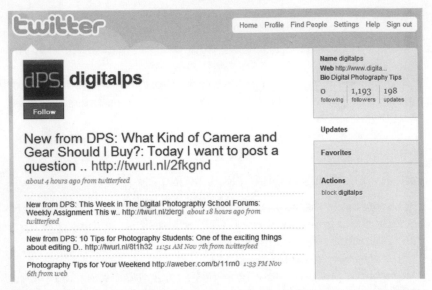

Figure 5.9   Could Darren Rowse's photography tweets be simpler? And yet they're making him money.

That's almost a 10 percent conversion rate from doing absolutely nothing at all.

In fact that means you can actually guesstimate how much each of those tweets is worth.

Now, I don't know what Darren's figures really are, but if he's converting three percent of his users into revenue through advertising, and generating, let's say one dollar from each ad click (he has a very well-respected site in a high-value field), then each tweet gives him about three dollars in direct revenue.

With 20 tweets visible on one page, each Twitter page then would represent about $60 worth of income in the space of just over a month.

That's not a huge amount of money, but it's completely effort-free. Once the Twitter account has been opened and the Wordpress plugin installed, Darren doesn't have to do anything more and he's just picked up an extra $50 or so a month in direct revenue.

Again, I don't know if these figures are true. That's not the point. The point is that you can actually calculate the value of your tweets—and you can earn directly from them too.

So how do you create tweets like these?

The easiest method is to do exactly what Darren did. He uses Twitterfeed, a service which checks his blog's RSS feed at set times and sends the title, description or both of any posts uploaded since its last check, together with a shortened link, through Twitter.

You can sign up for Twitterfeed at Twitterfeed.com. It's completely free and very easy to use, but you will need to have an RSS feed already set up on your site.

Once you've logged in—the service uses OpenID, so you can sign in using the same username and password that you've created at any one of a number of different sites—you'll be asked for your Twitter username and password; the URL of your RSS feed, how often you want Twitterfeed to check for new content; and how many updates you want to add at a time.

... feed your blog to twitter

Create new [twitter ▾] **feed**

Username: [ ]   Password: [ ]   test twitter authentication

RSS Feed URL: [http://]   test rss feed

Update frequency: [Every hour ▾]   **Post up to** [5 ▾] **new updates each time**
[Update Frequency describes how often we check your feed for new posts. The very first time we check, we post the most recent entry only, and after that, any new entries since the last time we checked.]

Include ... [title & description ▾]
☑ Include item link (if unchecked, sends tweet without the link)   Shorten link through [TinyURL ▾]

Post new items based on [pubDate ▾]

Prefix each tweet with: [ ]   (max. 20 characters)

Filter by keywords: [no filter]

☑ Active (if unchecked, this twitterfeed will be inactive, and will not post to twitter)

[Create] Cancel

Figure 5.10 Twitterfeed turns your blog posts into tweets automatically.

You should be a little careful here. If you have the sort of blog that has new RSS content shooting out several times a day, then your timeline is going to be filled with posts. It's going to look like a broadcast station.

Posting one article to your blog a day and letting Twitterfeed send one link tweet each day should be enough, especially if you're surrounding those tweets with other types.

Twitterfeed will also ask whether you want to include the post's title, description, or both; how to shorten the link; and whether to order the tweets according the site's publication date or the Globally Unique Identifier (GUID).

Include both the title and the description. Yes, it means that your tweet will be more than 140 characters, and that's bad etiquette. But the content itself is more than 140 characters, so by offering the first few words of the article, you'll create curiosity. If your followers want to find out what the rest of the sentence says, they'll have to click the link.

It's harder to generate that sort of interest with just a title that fits into the tweet space.

There are a number of different services that shorten URLs so that you don't end up filling the tweet with your post's address. They all do more or less the same thing, so choosing TinyURL keeps things nice and simple, and unless you have a good reason to do otherwise, publish your posts by publication date. Twitter's users expect updates to be chronological, so it's a good idea to keep to that format.

Finally, you have 20 characters to introduce the title, description, and link. Darren Rowse uses "New from DPS:" which is straightfor-

---

New from DPS: What Kind of Camera and Gear Should I Buy?: Today I want to post a question .. http://twurl.nl/2fkgnd

about 20 hours ago from twitterfeed

Figure 5.11 Darren Rowse's Twitterfeed tweets are longer than 140 characters and are cut in midflow. But they do create curiosity.

ward and effective, but you can also try leaving this blank and just deliver the RSS text as tweet content together with the link.

Test both approaches, track the results and see which produces more clicks.

And Twitterfeed also lets you filter content so that it only tweets about posts that contain certain keywords. You might want to use this if your blog's topics are broader than the interests of your followers but bear in mind that you can only include content, not exclude. It's almost inevitable, then, if you do choose to filter your content that you'll miss at least some posts.

The alternative to using Twitterfeed—or a similar service—is to write the tweets manually. That will give you complete control over when you update, but it will require a little more effort. Be sure to use a URL-shortening service to keep the link short and memorable.

There is a risk involved in using this method though. Darren's photography blog is interesting enough—and well-known enough—for people to want to follow his automated tweets just to stay informed. It's little different from following an RSS feed. But you can't rely on this method if the site doesn't have its own pulling power already. Few people are going to be attracted by a headline from a firm it hardly knows.

Dell, for example, has multiple Twitter accounts allowing each of its business branches to target separate markets. Whether you're following Direct2Dell (twitter.com/direct2dell), Dell Cloud Computing (twitter.com/dellintheclouds), Dell Small Business (twitter.com/DellSmallBiz), or Dell Your Blog (twitter.com/dellyourblog), all you're going to receive is Twitterfeed headlines from that business's blog.

The result is that even a company the size of Dell struggles to gain more than 150 followers on each of its Twitter accounts.

Of course, your own blog URLs aren't the only kind of links you can include in your tweets. You can add links to any sites that you've

I'm afraid! I'm so very afraid! - http://tinyurl.com/4m2ejk - Click at your own risk *about 17 hours ago from web*

Figure 5.12 Giving my followers fun with a link tweet.

found interesting and, more importantly, that you think your users would find interesting.

You can even send links to the articles you're reading at the moment.

This will mean that you're sending people away from your time-line, but they're going to leave anyway. It's much better that they leave with the impression that you're up-to-date with the latest news on your topic and that you're a source of great information.

CLASSIC TWEETS: "THIS IS WHAT I'M DOING NOW."

It's unlikely that you're going to get many replies to link tweets. Your followers will click the link, leave and by the time they remember they want to tell you what they think of the post, they're already long gone.

You might receive a few replies but on the whole, these are broadcast posts that are intended to be informative rather than updates that you can expect to provoke discussion.

But these could well be the only type of tweets that are purely one-way. As long as your followers are staying on your timeline, there's always the chance that someone will have a comment to make.

That's true even when you write the most basic of tweets, the one that Twitter suggests and for which the site was created: when you tell people what you're doing right now.

These are always going to be among the easiest types of tweets to create, and they're not hard to make interesting. Try to steer clear of

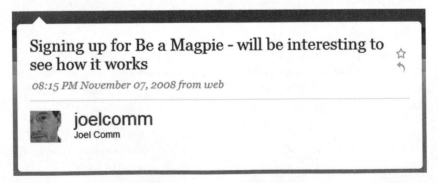

Signing up for Be a Magpie - will be interesting to see how it works

08:15 PM November 07, 2008 from web

joelcomm
Joel Comm

Figure 5.13   Don't just tell us what you're doing; tell us what you think about what you're doing too.

describing what you're eating. Too many people do this and unless you're traveling through the Sahara desert and dining on camel meat and toasted scorpions, that's going to get old very quickly. Focus on the various activities that you do during the day.

But here's the thing.

Don't just say: "Heading to the library" or "About to take a nap." *Also say what you think about what you're doing or explain why you're doing it.*

That makes the tweet so much more interesting.

The benefit of these kinds of tweets is that they let your followers follow you through the day. That's the idea of Twitter. It's a bit like reality TV, but you can choose from millions of lives to follow instead of the odd people the producers cram into the Big Brother house.

Just telling people exactly what you're doing then can be interesting, but talking to your followers about what you're doing is a little like stepping into the video booth and taking them into your confidence.

It has a much more powerful binding effect and is far more entertaining.

So a tweet that might have said "Heading to the library" becomes "Heading to the library to grab two kids' books for E. If I read The Gruffalo one more time, my head will explode."

And even "About to take a nap" would become "About to take a nap. Fingers already half-asleep. Summertime always does this to me."

Do you see how posts like these add personality to your timeline?

They don't just announce what you're doing. They describe who you are too.

When you're competing for the attention of followers from among millions of other Twitterers, it's these little details that can help you to stand out.

OPINION TWEETS: "THIS IS WHAT I'M THINKING NOW."

Okay, Twitter doesn't actually ask this, and there are even some Twitter purists who feel that tweets should only be about actions, not opinions.

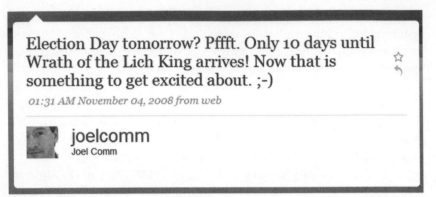

Election Day tomorrow? Pffft. Only 10 days until Wrath of the Lich King arrives! Now that is something to get excited about. ;-)

01:31 AM November 04, 2008 from web

joelcomm
Joel Comm

Figure 5.14 Sheesh...it's just an opinion...

I think they're wrong; that's my opinion.

Just as you can make tweets about actions more interesting when you also state your thoughts about those actions, so you can make your timeline more personal when you include tweets that describe what you think.

Anyone who has read my tweets and my blog knows that I'm not someone who is afraid to state my opinion. I have lots of them, they're strongly held—and lots of people don't agree with them.

That's fine. They don't have to read them.

I understand that telling people what I think about the various issues that concern me deeply might put some people off following me and reading my blog posts. It could cost me customers.

I'm prepared to accept that, but I don't think it's happening. On the contrary, I think that my openness and the fact that my readers know where I stand and what I think—even if they don't always agree with me—has a positive effect on the whole. The people I lose by expressing my opinions are made up for by the close connection I have with the readers and followers who remain.

That's always a choice you have to make when expressing an opinion, especially on controversial issues and especially when you're using Twitter for marketing. If you're marketing a corporate brand rather than a personal brand, for example, it might be a good idea to keep the opinions focused on topics that affect your industry.

People without opinions look impersonal; companies without opinions look impartial.

If you are using Twitter to reinforce your personal brand, feel free to share your thoughts on anything that comes to mind.

Tell people what you think of something that affects your industry.

Tell them what you think of something that's happening in the news.

Tell them what you think of something someone else posted.

Use tweets to tell people what you think about anything, and you'll be putting your personality into timeline.

MISSION ACCOMPLISHED TWEETS: "THIS IS WHAT I'VE JUST DONE."

Share your thoughts, and you're almost guaranteed to get people sharing theirs. Few things can start a discussion faster than expressing an opinion on a subject that you know lots of other people feel strongly about.

Telling people what you've just done can have the same effect.

These kinds of tweets look like broadcasts. They're really not much different from tweets that announce that you've just uploaded a new blog post.

Both talk about activities that you've already completed.

But while your followers can see the results of your link tweets, they won't always be able to see the results of your Mission Accomplished tweets. They'll only be able to comment on them.

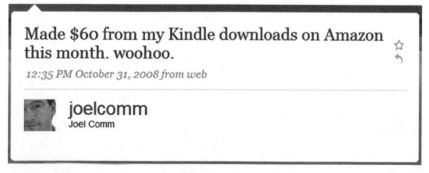

Made $60 from my Kindle downloads on Amazon this month. woohoo.

12:35 PM October 31, 2008 from web

joelcomm
Joel Comm

Figure 5.15   Mission accomplished!

Announcing that "I've just done this" is also another way of saying "What do you think of this?"

And the result is often answers to a question you didn't know you were asking. That's particularly true when the task you've accomplished is particularly interesting or impressive.

Tell people that you just broke $1,000 in monthly AdSense earnings, for example, and you can be confident that one of your followers will congratulate you . . . and ask you how you did it.

Tell them you just leveled up in World of Warcraft, and you could get a similar response.

And tell them that you've just baked a chocolate cake and that you're about to cut into a slice with a cup of coffee and the newspaper, and you'll probably get people asking you if they could have some too.

Tweeting about what you've done might be an odd way to answer the question "what are you doing now?" but it can be a very good way to fill your timeline.

ENTERTAINMENT TWEETS: "I'M MAKING YOU LAUGH NOW."

Followers follow people whose tweets they find informative, but they also follow people whose tweets they find entertaining. Stephen Fry's tweets, for example, are filled with the sorts of witty comments and insights that gave him a career as a comedy actor. Reading them is like watching one of his television shows . . . in 140-character bites.

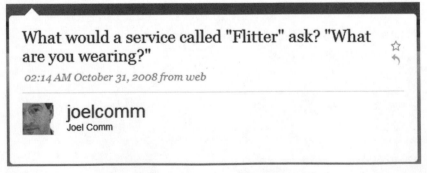

Figure 5.16   Okay, so I won't give up the day job . . .

If you can come up with tweets that are fun and entertaining to read, as well as being genuinely helpful, then you'll never struggle to find followers.

Ideally, of course, all of your tweets would be filled with jokes, humor, or wit. If you can't manage that, though, then depending on the subject of your timeline—and your ability to crack jokes—tossing in the odd humorous tweet can help to lighten the mood and make your Twitter page a fun space to hang out.

QUESTION TWEETS: "CAN YOU HELP ME DO SOMETHING NOW?"

One very easy way to turn your followers from readers into contributors is to ask a question. Twitterers do this often, tossing out requests for help from anyone in their follower list who might have some good advice.

Often, the questions will be very simple—ideas for birthday presents, recipes for tonight's dinner, etc. Sometimes, they can be fairly complex and demand expert help from people with specialized knowledge.

But questions don't just have to be requests for information. They can also be discussion starters. Ask your followers what they think about a topic, and you'll soon know just how engaged your followers really are—especially if you throw in your opinion first.

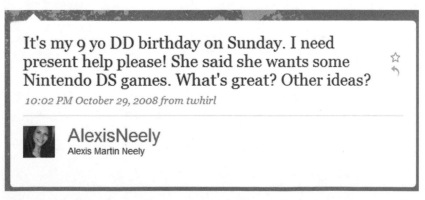

Figure 5.17 Legal expert and marketer Alexis Martin Neely (twitter.com/alexisneely) puts out a call for help.

Tweeting "I can't stand violent video games" could you get a discussion started in response.

Tweeting "What do you think of violent video games?" could have a similar effect.

But getting the discussion rolling by tweeting "My son plays violent video games. I can't stand them. What do you think?" increases the chances that your followers will hit the reply button and toss in their two cents.

PICTURE TWEETS: "LOOK AT WHAT I'VE BEEN DOING."

The short text updates that Twitter offers make both reading and contributing quick, letting users dip in and out. The investment in time and effort is small but the rewards can be much, much bigger.

Not surprisingly, Twitterers have been looking for ways around those restrictions. Including a link that takes the follower to a Web site is one simple way to do that, but you can also add a picture to your tweets.

Or rather, you can put a picture on the Web and send a tweet about it. True, that's not quite the same thing as attaching a photo to a message in the same way that you can do on Facebook or

sims

Follow

check out my new disney park wall: http://twitpic.com/nxb1 now i need maps from the international parks!!

9 minutes ago from TweetDeck

Figure 5.18   Andrew Sims (twitter.com/sims) shows off his desk.

MySpace, but it can still be a neat way to add content to your time-line, show people what you've been doing rather than tell them in 140 characters, and create new discussion points.

In theory, you can do this any way you want. There's no reason why you couldn't post an image to your Flickr stream and then add the link to a tweet. But TwitPic (www.twitpic.com) does make it all a great deal easier.

Sign in with your Twitter username and password, choose an image to upload, describe and tag it, then add a message on the same form that will be broadcast as a tweet. The tweet then appears in your timeline with a link to the image on TwitPic.

It's very neat, very simple and a very good way to share one more type of information with your followers.

Twitter asks a very simple question, and the answers it receives to that question have turned it into an Internet phenomenon. But one of the reasons that the site managed to expand so quickly is that its users have expanded the scope of its activities too.

Top Twitterers don't just explain what they're doing now. They also reveal what they've *been* doing, would like to do, and what they're thinking as well. They make their followers laugh, think,

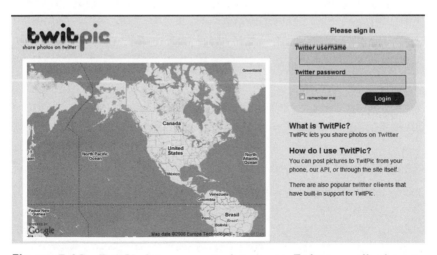

Figure 5.19   TwitPic lets you put pictures on Twitter—well, almost.

read, and above all, respond—and they do it with a variety of different kinds of tweets.

In this section, I've described some of the tweets that I use to
keep my followers engaged, and some of the tweets that I've seen
other Twitterers using too.

You don't have to use all of these different kinds of tweets.
Darren Rowse's digital photography school timeline does fine with
just one type. On the whole, I think you're going to get the best
results when you mix things up.

That should give you a social atmosphere in which you're the
host, free to make announcements and share your news.

There is one type of tweet that you *shouldn't* post though: the
kind of tweet that gets you in trouble.

We've all heard about people who have created videos of
themselves doing stupid things then posted them on YouTube for
everyone—including their boss—to see.

The same thing has happened on Twitter.

When PR executive Steve Rubel (twitter.com/steverubel)
tweeted that he had a free subscription to *PC Mag* but always
tossed it directly into the trash, the magazine's publishers weren't
too happy.

As they were his clients, they were also in a position to do something about it—and that short tweet left a big hole in his income.

Twitter may sometimes feel like a private space in which you're
just shooting the breeze with your pals, but it's not. People read it,
so if there's anything you don't want everyone and their uncle to
know, don't tweet it.

There are plenty of other ways to write enticing tweets without
landing yourself in hot water.

How to Drive Behavior

So far I've been focusing largely on one particular type of follower
response to your tweets. While some tweets simply provide information, others will spark a discussion in which your followers with
provide information of their own in return, spreading your name
across the Twitterverse and giving you a community.

But sometimes you want your followers to do other things.

Usually, that means clicking a link, but it rarely stops there. Once your follower has reached the Web site, you'll need to do something to monetize them, or at least start the process of monetizing them.

Your ability to do that will clearly depend far more on what that Web site says than on what a 140-character tweet says, but what you say on Twitter can have an effect on what the follower does eventually. Especially if you write the right kind of tweets.

We've already seen, for example, how t-shirt firm SpringLeap gets its users not just to visit its online store but to buy something when they get there by handing them a discount code on the way to the link. And they create urgency by making it clear that the code has a limited lifespan, increasing the chances that the follower will actually use it.

Discount cards and a time-limited offers are just two classic ways that you can influence follower behavior. Another method is to use spontaneity. Because Twitter happens in real time, you can decide to interact with your followers on the spur of the moment.

Anyone who's following your tweets at that particular moment gets to join in the fun and feel the benefits.

Anyone who stops by later will feel that they missed an opportunity and realize that they should be following you more often.

Sometimes, for example, I'll decide to do a live uStreamed broadcast from my office. During a visit from another marketing guru, we'll turn on the video camera and bring our Twitter audiences into our discussion by announcing it on the site.

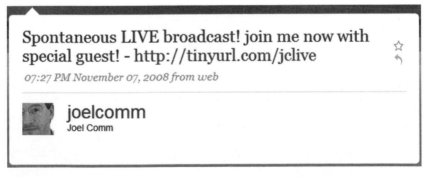

Figure 5.20 And on today's special edition of The Joel Comm Show...

When followers understand that this is a one-off surprise chance to pick up some valuable information, there's a good chance that they'll tune in.

Ultimately though, while your tweets can create interest, excitement and anticipation, they can only do so much. The real conversion work comes when they reach your Web page, which is why you must have your sales channels ready and set up before you drive your followers toward them.

But direct sales aren't the only way you can benefit from a long list of engaged followers. In the next chapter, I'm going to look at what talking to your customers on Twitter can do for you.

6

The Magic of Connecting with Customers on Twitter

When you produce interesting tweets, your followers benefit.

They find their way to your site where they can pick up some valuable information.

They enjoy the benefits of special offers and discount codes.

They gain a greater understanding of the sort of products, services, and information you provide.

They feel that they are part of a community that shares even more useful information and that provides support too.

And they can have a good time as well.

But a solid group of followers is also a resource for you, and not just because some of those followers will go ahead and make purchases either from you or from your sponsors. They're valuable because they're a giant source of information.

They're a source of information about your market and your products.

They're a source of information about who's talking about you, spreading your name, and winning you referrals.

And they're a source of information about all sorts of things that can help you to improve your products and grow your business.

In this chapter, I'm going to explain how Twitterers are using the site to build a focus group of customers that they can draw on to increase their bottom line.

Identifying Problems and Soliciting Feedback

The people who choose to follow you on Twitter are your most dedicated customers. They're the ones who want to be the first to know when you release a new product. They want to know what you're planning next, to pick up discounts that will cut the cost of their next purchase, and to lend you a hand, too.

Many of your followers will be such enthusiasts that they'll want to have an influence over your products, your blog posts, or the direction of your company.

They want to contribute. All you have to do is take advantage of that offer of help.

One way to do that is to give your followers a sneak peek before a major release and ask what they think.

Your followers will love this. They'll understand that they're being told about a new product before anyone else. That will make them feel part of an exclusive club.

When they tweet you back with their comments, you'll get to identify problems, bugs, and areas of improvement before you take the product public. You'll also get to build up interest so that when you do hit the release date, you've already primed the market, and you'll be able to use their praise as testimonials that you can include on your sales page.

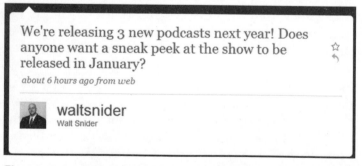

Figure 6.1   Podcaster Walt Snider (twitter.com/walt snider) rewards his followers with a sneak peek...and puts himself in line for some valuable feedback too.

When Internet marketer Thomas C. Gajdjis (twitter.com/ tommygadget) wrote a sales page for his e-book about blog flipping, for example, he wanted to know whether his copy looked compelling. The usual way to do that is to put up different pages and compare the results over time. Thomas, though, was able to ask his followers what they thought about his copy so that he could iron out any bumps before the launch.

He was also sending his followers to his sales page, making them aware that he was about to release a new book on a topic that they or their own readers might find interesting. Perhaps most importantly, when those followers replied, their followers would be alerted to his sales page too.

That's very simple. You don't have to do any more than make what you want examined available and then send out a tweet. You'll get a ton of very valuable feedback.

But this is another time to remember that Twitter is a public forum. When your followers hit the "reply" button to tell you what they think, they're also going to be telling their followers what they think.

That could be valuable marketing. It will help to spread the word about your launch. But that word-of-mouth marketing is only going to be helpful if your product is almost ready anyway. If you need to make a lot of corrections before you start selling, then that second ring of followers is going to see a great deal of criticism and very little praise. That's not likely to lead to sales.

If the product for which you want feedback is almost ready, then ask your followers to "reply." Everyone will see their response.

Is the sales copy a disaster, or does it rock? Go ahead, do your worst! *about 3 hours ago from web*

Go look at www.blogflippingfool.com and tell me what you think of the new site. Is it compelling? Good? Bad? Please check it out! Thanks. *about 3 hours ago from web*

Hello Twitters! Who's out there who can do me a really quick favor? I want you guys to tell me what you think of something. *about 3 hours ago from web*

Figure 6.2   Marketer Thomas C. Gajdjis puts his followers to work.

If you think the product or the sales page might still need a lot of work, ask them to direct message or e-mail you. You won't get the viral marketing, but you will get some valuable, relatively confidential feedback.

The drawback to picking up comments in this way is that any feedback you receive is likely to be short. If you're asking people to reply, they're not going to do more than identify one or two elements that could be changed and point them out in 140 characters or less.

If you're asking them to e-mail you, you might get a longer report, but you're still not likely to get a huge amount of detail. Your followers will want to be helpful, but few of them are going to invest a huge amount of time in improving your product or your sales copy.

Unless you ask them a ton of detailed questions.

When I was putting together this book, I wanted to know how people were using Twitter and what they wanted to do with the site. I could have simply sent out a tweet that asked, "Thinking of writing a book about marketing with Twitter. What would you like to see in it?" but I don't think I would have received many replies.

Instead, I used my company's survey software, InstantFormPro (www.instantformpro.com), to create a short questionnaire that guided my followers' responses and gave me exactly the information I was looking for.

Obviously, I promoted the survey through tweets, and I even included it on my Twitter background.

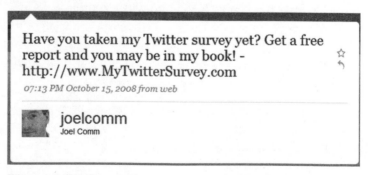

Have you taken my Twitter survey yet? Get a free report and you may be in my book! - http://www.MyTwitterSurvey.com

07:13 PM October 15, 2008 from web

joelcomm
Joel Comm

Figure 6.3 How to get masses of feedback for a project in the works.

Hundreds of people responded, and the survey gave me a huge amount of data. It also provided me with a valuable list of people who had expressed an interest in the subject.

As a method of generating detailed feedback as well as increased marketing range, surveys can be very powerful.

Discovering Your Top Fans, Promoters, and Evangelists

Read someone's Twitter timeline and it's going to feel a little like walking into a private party. The Twitterer will be replying to followers who replied to his tweets and addressing issues that other followers have raised.

There should be plenty of other interesting content there too, but much of the timeline of a good Twitterer will be directed at individuals.

Why those individuals? How do Twitterers choose which people to address and which to mention specifically, drawing the attention of all of their followers in turn to that Twitterer?

How *should* they choose them?

Often, a reply that drops a name in front of every other follower on a list will be a direct response to something that Twitterer said. Hit "reply" to a tweet, and there's a reasonable chance that the Twitterer will hit "reply" back. That's especially true if you've done your homework, read the timeline, and paid attention to the sorts of things that might catch a Twitterer's attention.

Notice that someone you follow replies to questions, for example, and you should get a reply with a good query. If they respond to praise, then a pat on the back could win you a spot on their timeline.

But there's another reason that a twitterer could—and should—mention one of his followers in his timeline: if that follower is one of his key marketers.

Every good business has people like this. They're your most loyal customers, the ones who rave about your products to their friends, send links to your articles to their contact list, and are always getting in touch with questions, suggestions, and feedback.

Those people are worth gold to any business, and good marketers will want to do everything they can both to keep them happy and to make the most of them.

Twitter lets you do both. And it helps you to find them too.

In fact, there are all sorts of ways to discover who is talking about you the most on Twitter—and companies are using them.

In September 2006, for example, *BusinessWeek* described how Twitterer Jonathan Fields (twitter.com/jonathanfields) had spotted William Shatner boarding a JetBlue flight at New York's JFK airport earlier that year. He sent out a tweet that wondered aloud why the actor was flying a budget airline—and immediately received an e-mail saying that JetBlue was now following him on Twitter.

The company had been alerted to its name in a tweet and responded by following a customer who had already shown that he was prepared to talk about the airline.

There are a number of ways to do that.

One method is simply to toss your username into Twitter's search engine at search.twitter.com and see who comes up. You will be able to count who has mentioned you the highest number of times in their tweets and who is giving you the most praise.

But search will only tell you who has been talking about you in the past. Unless you leave it open in your browser and refresh the page constantly, it won't tell you who is talking about you now.

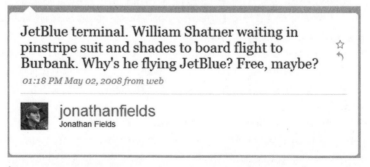

Figure 6.4 Jonathan Fields spots Captain Kirk boarding a JetBlue plane. JetBlue spots the reference and hones in on a customer.

Twitter does have a tracking system that can do that. Type "track [keyword]" into your instant messenger or mobile device and every time someone types that keyword—such as your "@username"—in a tweet, you'll receive a message telling you what they said.

You'll then be able to check out who they are or reply to their tweet.

That's one useful way to stay informed about what people are saying about you, but not everyone uses a mobile device with their Twitter account, and when you're tracking to discover your biggest evangelists, you also want to be able to keep records of what people are saying.

That will enable you to create detailed lists of who is generating referrals on your behalf, which topics interest them the most, and what is most likely to spark a retweet or a reply.

A better method is to use a service called Monitter (www .monitter.com). This lets you keep track of three different keywords

Figure 6.5   Twitter's search engine gives me a list of people who have been talking about me. Brian Willms (twitter .com/brianwillms) is the CEO of my local Chamber of Commerce. He's a very nice guy and it looks like he's very well-read too.

Figure 6.6   TweetBeep keeps your ear to the ground, letting you know who's saying what about you.

in real time. It's fun, but you can't keep the tweets permanently, so unless you're watching it all the time and making notes, you will lose some people.

The best way to keep track of what people are saying about you, your product, or even your industry, then, is to use TweetBeep (tweetbeep.com).

This works in exactly the same way as Google's Alert service. Sign up and you'll be able to enter keywords that you want to follow. TweetBeep will search for them every hour or every day, depending on your choice, and send you an e-mail every time it comes across a new mention of that term.

Set up filters in your e-mail client and you'll soon have all of your keywords arranged into folders, so that you can see which Twitterers are most interested in the topics your business covers.

You could have one alert—and one folder—for tweets that mention your username. Another alert could cover mentions of your business's name. Another could look for mentions of your blog, and another the title of your e-book, your main product, or your topic, and so on.

That will give you all the data you need to create list of the most important—and active—Twitterers in your field.

Now you have to act on that data.

Obviously, the first thing you should do is to make sure that you're following those Twitterers. They're going to be tweeting about all sorts of other topics too, but because these people are of interest to you, you'll want to know what they're saying.

This is exactly what Twitter is for.

You'll then want to start bringing them into your conversation.

If they haven't replied to one of your tweets already, then start by introducing yourself. Find one of their tweets to reply to and offer some good information.

Even if they've only mentioned your subject rather than your name or one of your products, there's still a good chance that they'll know who you are, so it shouldn't be difficult to get them to follow you and to start building up a relationship.

And once you have that relationship, you'll want to make the most of it. Before you release a new product, reply to your top evangelists to ask them what they think.

Give them sneak peeks of what you're doing so that they'll rush off and tell their friends.

When you see that they've left a great recommendation for you in a tweet, direct message them to give them a bonus reward.

When they mention that they bought your latest product or that they're reading your blog post, drop them a line to ask what they think. They'll be thrilled, and you'll get a testimonial on their timeline.

When you can see who is saying nice things about you—and what they're saying—you can take all sorts of steps to encourage them and keep them spreading the word.

If they're saying good things, it's like having a constant stream of referrals and recommendations right on your profile page.

Your Micro Help Desk

Your evangelists and promoters are people who are going to be helping you anyway. They do that because they like your business. They're excited about it, they enjoy the benefits it brings, and they want their friends to share those benefits too.

Only a small number of your followers are going to fit into this category, though. The rest are just going to be people who are interested in what you do and want to know what you're doing now.

But those people can still bring you a huge amount of value.

We've already seen how they can help you to spot problems before you launch products. But they can also help you in all sorts of other ways. Because the site is filled with experts who possess all sorts of specialized knowledge, Twitter can be a one-stop help desk for whatever you're struggling with.

The easiest way to find help is simply to ask the people you know if they can supply it.

Obviously, this is always going to work best when you have a giant follower base. The higher the number of people following your tweets, the greater the chances that one of them will be able to lend a hand.

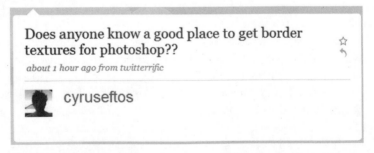

Figure 6.7 Cyruseftos (twitter.com/cyruseftos) puts out a call for help.

That means that as you're building your followers, it's worth paying attention to what each of them does and considering the sort of help they might be able to offer in the future.

Choose to follow a Web design expert, for example, and you should be picking up some interesting tweets that could help generate your own design ideas. But if you can get the designer to sign up as one of your followers, then when you ask a question about Web design, there's a good chance that you'll get a professional answer.

It's also worth looking at the number of followers your followers have. If you can get followed by a few people with large audiences, there's always a chance that your requests for help will be passed along or that their readers will click through to see your tweets.

Followers with lots of followers of their own can provide outlets to plenty of help.

So how do you ask for that help?

You could certainly come straight out and ask if anyone knows a skilled programmer or a great copywriter or where you can get a good logo designed.

That would be very simple, and depending on the size and make-up of your followers, there's a very good chance that it would give you results.

You could also ask your followers to retweet your message to help you find the assistance you need.

And again, every time you do this, you're spreading your name across the Twitterverse. People like to help, and they like to show off their own expertise too, so when someone tweets back with the information and advice you were looking for, you get to appear in their timeline and they get to look like an expert.

Everyone wins.

But Twitter isn't the best place to find the help you need for your business.

Conferences are much better.

I'm a huge fan of conferences. I think they're fantastic places to learn new skills, become aware of outstanding opportunities, and meet other entrepreneurs keen on starting joint ventures and bursting with ideas.

I don't understand why everyone doesn't go to a conference.

I do understand why everyone doesn't go to *every* conference. That would take far too much effort.

One of the most effective uses for Twitter then, is to follow tweets from people attending conferences.

That's never going to be as effective as being there in person, but it is still valuable.

If you know someone—or even better, a group of people—who are attending a conference, make sure that you're following their tweets. You should be able to pick up an idea of what people are saying, the sorts of advice the speakers are offering, and the questions people are asking.

It might even be possible to tweet back with your own questions for someone at the conference to ask on your behalf.

I still think that you should be attending conferences. But if there are some that you can't make, Twitter can help you to get a taste of what you're missing—and tap a truly expert source.

Both of these approaches though are about you extracting help from your followers. That's valuable, but it works the other way too.

Yes, you should be offering solutions whenever you see people asking questions in your field. We've already seen how that can be a great way to win followers and show off your own skills.

But it's even more important that you supply help that's directly related to your business.

This is where tracking keywords related to your business is so important.

It would be nice to believe that every tweet that mentions the name of your business is going say what a great company you have, how awesome your products are, and that absolutely everyone should buy absolutely everything you're selling. Then buy some more for their families.

But life just isn't like that.

Inevitably, you're going to see tweets from people who just weren't happy.

Some of them won't be happy with the quality of the product. They'll find that it didn't do what they hoped it would do—even if their hopes were way off base.

Others will complain about the customer service. For some people, if they don't get a refund because they're not still using

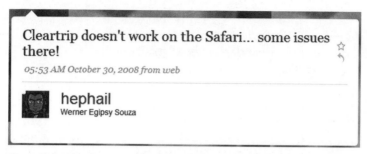

Figure 6.8 Cleartrip (twitter.com/cleartrip), an Indian travel firm, uses its followers as an unpaid quality assurance team.

a product four years after buying it, something's wrong with the company.

And for others, they'll have encountered a bug, a mistake, or an inaccuracy that they want to highlight.

Whatever the reason, whenever you see a complaint that relates to your product, jump on it.

Ask them what the problem is. Show that you're prepared to work with them to try to fix it. And when you do fix it, let them know by sending them a reply tweet so that everyone can see.

When you do that, you pick up a number of important benefits.

You stop that bad publicity in its tracks. If positive viral marketing can have fantastic effects on your sales, negative tweets can seriously restrict your growth.

You also get to turn a complainer into an unpaid member of your quality assurance team.

That old saying "the customer is always right" might not always be right (sometimes the customer is just plain wrong, but it's right not to tell him!), but you can always learn something from a customer complaint.

When ClearTrip (twitter.com/cleartrip), an online travel firm in India, noticed a tweet that mentioned the site wasn't working in Safari, for example, its staff was fast to ask what was going wrong so that they could fix the problem.

The risk here is that your Twitter account will morph into an always-on customer help desk. Rather than broadcasting the

@hephail please let us know what issues you
faced with Safari, it is one of our favourite
browsers and we do our best to support it

03:43 PM November 06, 2008 from web in reply to hephail

 cleartrip

Figure 6.9   Hephail (twitter.com/hephail) spots a problem
with a product. The company spots his complaint and acts
on it.

messages you want to put out, you'll be spending much of your
Twitter time telling people how to solve their problems and following up bug reports.

But perhaps that's no bad thing. ClearTrip also has a corporate
Twitter account, and its staff have accounts too. Twitter itself sends
out tweets that announce error reports and keep its 35,839 followers
informed about what's happening on the site, while its staff are free
to tweet their personal stuff without being disturbed.

Because there's no limit on the number of Twitter accounts you
can set up, you could create a separate account that functioned as
an online, real-time help desk.

Your customers would know where to come for help, and everyone would see that you're dedicated to meeting their demands.

Twitter is as much a conversation tool as broadcasting device.
Used carefully, you can have fantastic chats with your customers
and your clients.

You can have conversations that help you spot problems before
your product is released and to win feedback and reviews.

You can follow conversations so that you can see what people
are saying about you—and encourage them to keep on saying nice
things about you.

And you can talk to those people who are less than completely
happy, turning your Twitter account into the kind of open-access
help desk that your customers will love and your potential customers will appreciate.

But you can also use Twitter talk to your staff and your team.

That's what I'm going to discuss in the next chapter.

7

Leveraging Twitter for Team Communication

It's a conundrum. Twitter relies on tiny little posts, yet the effect is massive. It's certainly been massive for the people who created the site, but it's also huge for relationships between people. Now readers of my blog and followers of my tweets can see what I'm doing and what I'm thinking throughout the day.

Instead of relying on an occasional blog post, they get brief updates that, because they only take a second to write, come in on a regular basis.

Now I'm not a distant friend who sends occasional letters. I'm the guy in the next office they pass in the corridor.

That makes a huge difference to the way any online entrepreneur interacts not only with his customers but also with anyone else involved in his business.

I have a beautiful office in Loveland, Colorado, staffed with some great people. But I also employ freelancers scattered around the country and even around the world. It's one of the benefits of the digital age: I can hire the best people for the job, wherever they may be.

Some of those people have been working with me for years. I've never met them and I can count on the fingers of half a hand the number of times I've spoken on the phone to some of them. Lots of other entrepreneurs do the same thing, and plenty of people today consider their local coffee shop to be their prime working space.

These days you don't need to be in the same office as someone working on the same project to get the task done. As long as everyone has an Internet connection—and you can rely on them—your team members can be thousands of miles apart.

While telecommuting means you're not limited to your local labor pool, it does have its disadvantages. A team member you never see and never talk to can feel remote. The connection between you isn't the same as that between you and someone in the same building. They'll feel left out of the loop, and they won't be up to date with the changes happening in your company.

That means they'll be less able to help with those changes, and there's always the risk that they'll be left behind.

When you're all Twittering, though, it's much easier to see what everyone is doing.

You can see what they're working on, the team members can see what you're up to and you'll all feel much closer.

Twitter for Virtual Team Leaders

That means those tweets don't even have to be work-related. While a tweet that tells everyone in the team which aspect of the project they're building now will certainly be helpful, a quick note offering a prediction for the night's ball game or revealing what's in their grocery bag can be useful too.

That's because of Twitter's power as a virtual water cooler.

It's a place where people come to hang out, shoot the breeze, and talk about things that aren't really business-oriented at all.

And just as those sorts of random conversations make people feel closer to each other, so tossing out random thoughts on Twitter can have the same effect.

You could say what you're doing, add a link to a blog you're reading, or reply to someone else's tweet. The frequent reminders keep everyone in each other's minds and *the thoughts themselves let everyone understand who the writer is*.

This is important. Employees and team members don't just work for money. They also work for the satisfaction of the job they're doing. They stay with their current companies and continue working on their current projects because they find the challenge interesting and they like the people they're working with.

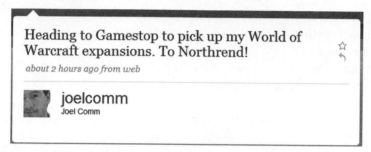

Figure 7.1 Now everyone knows I like computer games...

Those connections are as much a part of incentivizing workers as bonuses and options.

When your team is scattered and the members never meet, those connections are very weak. It becomes very easy for a team member to drift away and be tempted by another interesting project.

If loyalty can no longer be taken for granted at bricks-and-mortar companies, it certainly can't be assumed at firms connected only by e-mail.

On the other hand, when team members feel that they're working for a real person, alongside other real people—people who play video games, teach their kids soccer, cook lasagna on the weekends, etc.—they feel that they're part of a community. It becomes much harder to walk away. They're not betraying an e-mail; they're leaving a friend in the lurch.

You're likely to be sending these kinds of personal, informal tweets anyway.

You're also likely to be sending out tweets that announce blog updates or invite your followers to check out your new release. But those non-business tweets can have strong business effects.

Creating a Twitter Account for a Virtual Team

Making sure that your Twitter timeline includes at least some informal tweets will help you connect with your virtual team members. But it's not a strategy that's dedicated to the virtual team. Those team members will only form one part of your followers. As a result, they may feel a little like interlopers, watching the conversation from the outside.

If you want to really get them involved, you can try to bring them into your community by creating a dedicated Twitter account just for the team.

We've already seen how ClearTrip has both a corporate Twitter account and separate accounts that its employees use to communicate with customers.

There's no reason why a team leader couldn't create a Twitter account specifically for members of the team.

Each team member won't only feel that they're a member of an exclusive club. They'll also understand that they're working on something communal, rather than building something alone.

The risk though is that communication which might best be kept secure will find its way into the public. Just as you can monitor the conversations of people who mention your products, so your competitors would be able to follow what you're saying to your team members—unless you keep your tweets private.

Click the *Protect my updates* check button on the Settings page of your Twitter account, and only the people you approve will be able to follow your updates.

You're not going to have many followers on a timeline like this. And you're not going to be driving people to your commercial sites or to your blog. But that's not the point. You will have created an online forum where your team members can talk, interact, and keep everyone updated on the progress of the project.

There are some disadvantages here, though.

Twitter is still relatively new and it's not yet as well-known as Facebook. Not all of your team members are going to be familiar with the service or feel comfortable using it. You're likely to find that this strategy works best with people who already know how to use the system and do it anyway.

☐ Protect my updates

Only let people whom I approve follow my updates. If this is checked, you WILL NOT be on the public timeline.

[Save]

Figure 7.2 Protect your updates and your team chats will stay private.

And while it works in real time, you want your team members to be working on the project, not spending their time writing tweets!

Use a team Twitter account to troubleshoot problems, request help, and provide updates, but this is one time when you want to try to keep the tweets as professional as possible.

Building a Team with Twitter

So Twitter can help to keep together a team that's already been established. It can do that by helping scattered members to understand that they're working alongside each other and that they're not alone. And it can do it by providing an online clubhouse where they can get together to keep everyone informed.

But the site can also be used to put those teams together in the first place.

When you need help with your business, there are all sorts of places you can look. I've had a lot of luck with Elance, a job site for freelancers, but word of mouth, personal Web sites, and even friends and family can all be good sources of team members.

In fact, you're likely to be spoiled for choice—which is not a good thing. Choosing isn't easy, so you could find yourself wasting time trying to break in new team members, only to find that they don't make the grade and need to be replaced.

Figure 7.3   Virtual assistant Trudy Valencia (twitter.com/ estediava) uses Twitter to join the corporate team.

Twitter can make those hiring decisions a great deal easier.

The fact that someone is on Twitter is already a good sign. That shows that they're not scared of new technology and that they're used to communicating and staying in touch at a distance—all important considerations when you're building a virtual team.

But Twitter also reveals far more about that team member than you're likely to find on any resume or in any portfolio.

Of course, you'll want to read those too. The Twitterer's bio page should contain a link to their Web site, where you'll be able to see how they present themselves professionally. Need a designer, for example, and you'll be able to see their designs and gain an understanding of their style.

But there's more to working with someone than the quality of the work they deliver.

There's also the question of their reliability, their professionalism, their ability to keep to deadlines, their communication skills. . . and whether they're just a pleasant person to work with.

When you're hoping to work with someone over the long term, all of those elements are going to be important—and not all of them will be visible on their professional Web site.

Read their tweets, however, and you'll be able to see not just what their work is like, but what they're like too.

You can start with a search on Twitter's search engine, at search.twitter.com. Toss in a keyword that only a professional with the sort of skills you need is likely to use. If you were looking for a designer, for example, you could see who is using the term "raster."

If you were hunting for someone to help with your Web site, you could see who's been tweeting about "open source."

If you were looking for a copywriter to produce a sales page, you could search for terms such as "copy," "headline," or "call to action."

Clearly, not all of those people are going to be available for freelance work. But some will be, and you can add terms such as "freelance" or "contract" to narrow down the search.

Once you've managed to find a few freelancers with the skills you need, the fun can really begin. You'll be able to read their tweets to see how friendly they are and what they like to discuss.

There are a couple of things worth paying particular attention to.

First, note how often they answer questions.

Asking technical questions is nice—just knowing how to ask requires some knowledge—but more important is knowing how to answer. That demonstrates an even higher level of knowledge, and even more importantly, it also shows a willingness to help people with less knowledge than they possess themselves—and that, after all, is why you're hiring someone.

But note, too, how they use jargon. Are they comfortable with the technical terms? Do they appear to be familiar with the latest technology?

And even more importantly, look at who they're following and who's following them.

The best experts in each field are likely to have created their own communities of similarly skilled professionals. They might not have done that deliberately, but if they're tweeting about their profession and providing good information, there's a great chance that other professionals will be following them.

If you don't want to approach that professional—or if they're not available for hire—then following their own follow list could lead you to others.

This strategy works in reverse too.

Virtual assistant Trudy Valencia (twitter.com/estediava) uses Twitter to trawl the site for possible clients. When she finds people who have expressed an interest in outsourcing, she follows them and makes it clear that she's available to lend a hand.

It's a very simple formula that requires little more than careful searching, a polite approach, and the understanding that you're not going to win a job with every follow.

Twitter works wonderfully when used by individuals to broadcast information about themselves and to keep in touch with other individuals across the Twitterverse.

It can also be hugely beneficial to businesses relying on scattered teams, allowing them to create the kind of bonds that previously could only be formed in offices.

But Twitter is also used to build brands.

8

Using Twitter to Help Build Your Brand

Online advertising has really spoiled everyone. Not only can advertisers now finely target where their ads appear, making sure that they're only shown to people most likely to find them interesting, they can also track what happens after those ads go up.

They can measure how many people see the ads, how many click on them to learn more, and most importantly, how many actually buy as a direct result of seeing their commercial.

With that kind of targeting and data, it's no wonder that Google, with its leading AdSense system, is worth billions of dollars.

But the old advertising system didn't disappear. Drive down any highway, and you're still going to see giant billboards drawing your eye and advertising businesses.

Times Square still has its neon lights, and even TiVo hasn't rid television programs of commercial breaks every 10 minutes.

The Internet might have changed some of the ways that advertising works, but brand-building is still important. *If you want people to know who you are and remember the name of your business, you have to keep putting it in front of them, and you have to continue to interact with your buyers.*

That's what traditional advertising has always aimed to do. An advertiser who bought a radio spot in the 1950s wasn't expecting to see a spike in sales immediately after his ad was broadcast. But he was expecting to see his product's name recognition increase.

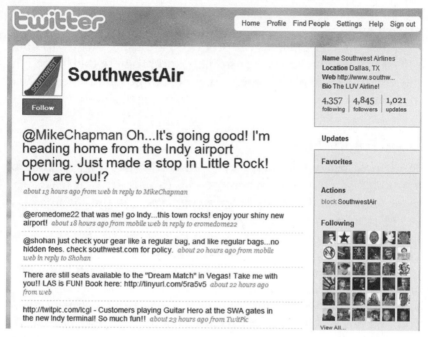

Figure 8.1 Southwest Airlines is just one company that uses Twitter to talk to customers and build a brand.

Customers would become familiar with the product and, over time, as they absorbed the advertising message, they'd trust it and they'd buy it.

On the Internet, that's been done with banner ads that keep a product's name visible at the top of a Web page, and with campaigns that pay for each 1,000 views rather than for each click that the ad receives.

And it can be done now with Twitter, too.

Twitter has proven a very valuable branding tool, and it hasn't been lost on many big corporations.

Just some of the companies you can find on Twitter include Carnival Cruise Lines (twitter.com/CarnivalCruise), Delta Airlines (twitter.com/deltaairlines), JetBlue (twitter.com/JetBlue), Dell (twitter.com/Direct2Dell), Amazon (twitter.com/amazondeals), Forrester (twitter.com/forrester), GM (twitter.com/GMblogs), and my favorite, M&Ms (twitter.com/msgreen and twitter.com/mmsracing).

All of these companies (or products) are using Twitter to build a loyal following with their customers and promote their brand. In this chapter, I'll explain some of the most important things to bear in mind when you do the same thing for your business.

Create a Story

At its most basic, branding can simply mean putting the name of a product or a company where people can see it. That makes the name familiar so that a customer recognizes it on the shelf.

In practice, of course, branding does much more than that. It also attaches the product's name to a story, so that when the customer sees it, he trusts it and associates with it.

It's that trust and attachment that are key to successful branding, and both start with a story.

Before you begin using Twitter to brand your company then, you first need to think about what you want that brand to say. Do you want your product to look cool and streetwise, or luxurious and exclusive? Do you want it be associated with ideas of health and nature, or would it sell better if customers considered it to be at the peak of technological development?

Take a look at how competing products sell themselves and decide how you want your product to appear in the market. Usually, rather than trying to create a brand from scratch, you'll be able to create a variation on a general theme used in your industry.

Internet marketers, for example, might be a pretty mixed bunch, but many of us like to appear in suits. That shows that while we might spend our days writing Web content and creating products, we're really traditional business people who broker deals and negotiate partnerships. We'll then try to mark ourselves out within that niche with a brand that represents our own unique personalities.

My Twitter page uses a pretty straightforward picture of me, and my bio describes me first as a husband and father. That down-to-earth image might accurately reflect who I am, but it's also a part of my brand. People know, when they read my blog, that I'm just a regular family guy with a good business who's prepared to share what he's learned.

Figure 8.2   Leading Internet marketer Yanik Silver (twitter .com/yaniksilver) creates an adventurous brand on Twitter.

My friend Yanik Silver, on the other hand, is much more of a daredevil. His bio includes the term "adventurer" and his photo shows him hanging over a computer like Tom Cruise in *Mission Impossible*. That action stuff is part of his brand—and a part of his story.

One product that does a very careful job of creating the right story for its market—and which also does it through Twitter—is M&Ms. By giving different colored candies different personalities, Mars, the manufacturer, is able to appeal to different kinds of buyers.

Twitter therefore, has a timeline for green M&Ms (twitter.com/ msgreen) which is targeted towards women, but it also has another timeline "written" by the red M&M (twitter.com/mmsracing) which associates itself with NASCAR to appeal to men. (The

Figure 8.3   M&Ms uses two types of brand images on Twitter. The green M&Ms are more popular.

mmsracing account has 96 followers, while the msgreen account, which has been online just six months longer, has 603 followers.)

It's likely that you already have a good idea of the kind of story you want your brand to portray. So how can you use Twitter to put that story across?

Portraying Your Brand with Your Profile

We saw earlier in this book how the background of the profile can be a useful way of providing your followers with more information than you can squeeze into a bio.

By creating a sidebar on the left of the page, you can send followers to your other Web sites, where they might be able to do a range of different things from clicking your ads to making purchases.

Those are direct results. When you're using Twitter to build a brand, though, you don't need your followers to type a URL into their browser or make a purchase right away. You just want them to remember you.

That means producing a design that makes your brand memorable and that sums up you or your company.

Southwest Airlines, for example, uses an image of its planes' tail as its photo and chose the sky as its background image. Readers can

Figure 8.4   M&M's old Twitter page used the green candy to push the brand in the run up to Valentine's Day. Note how they matched the color scheme and graphics with the subject of the campaign.

see immediately whose page they're reading and they understand what the company does.

Mars has gone a little further in its branding of M&Ms. Not only did the company create two pages, but it also changes the pages' designs so that the brand's image suits the current campaign. For Valentine's Day 2008, for example, the company used Twitter to promote the idea that green, not red, is the color of love—and that their green candies were symbols of love too. The profile used a green background with a picture of Eros as a green M&M, and the company's Web site linked to the Twitter page, where people could discover "love tips, quips, and personal appearances."

It was certainly memorable, and the image alone was enough to help the page to stand out.

But the profile doesn't have to be spectacular to convey the story of your brand, be instantly recognizable, and stick in the mind. Whole Foods Market (twitter.com/wholefoods), for example, simply uses a plain green background to match its green image and uses its logo as its picture.

That's very simple—and still very effective.

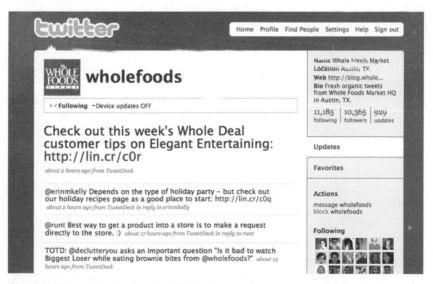

Figure 8.5   Whole Foods Market goes for green, pure and unadulterated, for its Twitter background.

When you're using Twitter for branding, then, your background image is going to be important. You can choose an image that's complex and carefully designed—and change it as you change your marketing—or you can opt for something very simple that still does the job.

More important is the style you use in your tweets.

Tweet Style: What to Say When You're Building a Brand to Create Value, and How to Say It

Jonathan Fields' response to being followed by an airline company minutes after tweeting about them wasn't completely positive. *BusinessWeek* quotes him as saying that he was "totally startled," and says that at first, he thought that JetBlue had noticed he was using the airport's wireless network.

The feeling was a mixture of respect for the company's diligence and use of technology . . . and general creepiness about the fact that they were watching him.

Clearly, there is a danger for companies using Twitter to communicate with customers and build their brand. When they put themselves in the public arena, there's a chance that they can do more harm than good. Firms that get social media wrong look like interlopers, uninvited guests who have gatecrashed the cool people's party.

That doesn't just mean that they're missing out on all of the opportunities that the social media site offers. It can also show that the company just doesn't "get it." That could have as negative an effect on their sales as good tweeting can have a positive effect.

There are a few things that the company needs to do to blend in on Twitter and make sure that the image it's putting across on the site strikes a chord.

The first thing it needs to do is to *be human*.

Comcast, for example, takes a huge amount of flack on Twitter. Twitterers are constantly complaining about the company's poor phone-based customer service.

No one though seems to be complaining about its Twitter-based customer service at twitter.com/comcastcares. It's run by Frank

Figure 8.6 Comcast shows that it cares by giving its tweets a human face.

Eliason, the "Director of Digital Care for Comcast," who puts his own picture rather than the company logo on the bio, includes an e-mail address for people to contact the company, and broadcasts tweets that look like they're coming from a Twitterer, not some company rep.

Note how the company puts together a whole bunch of different strategies here:

♦ It's chosen a name that doesn't just reflect the company but that refutes a common criticism made of the corporation on Twitter.

♦ It's used the background image to keep pushing that message home.

♦ Its tweets are written by a named individual who converses with the company's customers, and doesn't just broadcast messages to them.

♦ And it follows about the same number of people that follow its tweets to show that it's listening as well as talking.

As we'll see, these are characteristics that appear in the time-lines of many other successful companies on Twitter. They're also characteristics that are missing from companies that are really trying to make the most of Twitter . . . and failing.

Like Comcast, BestBuy (twitter.com/gina_community) also uses a real person rather than a logo to front its corporate Twitter page. Unlike Comcast though, BestBuy makes all sorts of mistakes that serve up a valuable lesson for any business thinking of using Twitter for branding.

First, the name is wrong. Twitter.com/bestbuy has been taken, but it has no updates, is following no one, and only has 26 followers. Twitter doesn't allow cybersquatting and has been known to take away accounts from individuals who tried to use a company name, so that URL should be available to BestBuy if they wanted it. It's possible that there is a good reason that the company doesn't want to use twitter.com/bestbuy . . . but I can't think of one.

Unless it's so that no one actually sees the profile picture.

While Frank Eliason looks happy, friendly, and approachable in his image, "Gina" looks like she's been locked in a hotel room with a laptop.

Worst of all, the tweets themselves consist of little more than cut-and-pasted statements made in response to alerts of the company name.

The overall impression isn't that this is a friendly, helpful company that wants to improve its customers' experience, but that this is a company that just doesn't care.

Figure 8.7   How not to build a brand on Twitter. BestBuy gets it all wrong with a poor image and creepy tweets.

The only consolation is that BestBuy has only managed to gather 166 followers—but that's likely to be 166 customers who have been put off by the tweet they've received.

Having a human—rather than a corporate—presence on Twitter might involve actually showing a human face in the way that Comcast does. But it will always involve tweeting in an *informal, friendly manner*.

Twitter, after all, is a very personal place. It's a site that asks a personal question and lets people share their random thoughts with the world at large.

Businesses that tweet like a corporate executive addressing a board meeting will stand out on the site and scream that they have no idea what they're doing—or who they're talking to.

Starbucks' (twitter.com/starbucks) timeline, for example, consists mostly of a customer representative answering questions. The company appears to be using the site as an extension of its customer service—one very simple corporate use for Twitter. It uses a logo instead of a personal image, but the employee responsible for managing the account isn't afraid to talk about his own personal experiences. He discusses the branches he's worked at and, of course, his own favorite drinks.

Although it's clear that this a corporate Twitter account, the tweets are written in a friendly, laid-back manner that creates the impression that the followers are chatting with the barista exactly as

Figure 8.8 Starbucks shows that it's a relaxed place to hang out with friendly, easygoing tweets.

they might do at the café itself—and that the café itself is a friendly, relaxed place to be.

That's good branding.

So your tweets should be friendly. They have to sound like they're coming from a real person, another member of the Twitter community, not from some creepy company that's listening out for a mention of their name.

But what should those tweets say to build a brand image that's positive and memorable?

In practice, corporate tweets that try to build brands tend to fall into four broad categories:

♦ Company news

♦ Customer support

♦ Feedback

♦ Special offers

News

We've already seen that only posting news updates on Twitter can make for a pretty ineffective timeline. Dell's tweets are dull tweets.

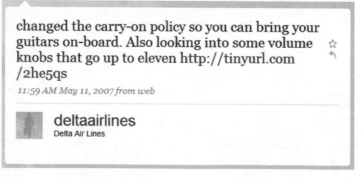

changed the carry-on policy so you can bring your guitars on-board. Also looking into some volume knobs that go up to eleven http://tinyurl.com /2he5qs

11:59 AM May 11, 2007 from web

deltaairlines
Delta Air Lines

Figure 8.9   Delta Airlines (twitter.com/deltaairlines) hasn't been updated for a while, but its tweets included important news about the company's carry-on policy ... and its corporate Twitterer added an important human touch too.

But including some carefully chosen news posts can have a positive branding effect. They reward the follower with useful information and they also show that the company is enthusiastic about what it's doing.

That enthusiasm can be infectious.

Clearly, you have to be careful to make sure that you're broadcasting the right kind of news and that you're doing it in the right way.

Usually one of the most important rules for releasing news about a company is whether it passes the "Who cares?" test.

In general, no one cares what companies are up to. If your local medical clinic had just repainted its waiting room, why would you care?

You wouldn't care unless that information actually affected you. If the clinic had changed its phone number or fired your doctor, then you'd want to know. If it's changed its design, you probably wouldn't want to know.

On Twitter, that rule still holds to some degree. News announcements that affect the reader are always going to be the most interesting. But even an announcement that a company has changed its blog design or squished another bug in its program can be interesting if it looks like gossipy fun.

The best way to handle news for branding, then, is to mix it in with other kinds of content and to add a personal comment

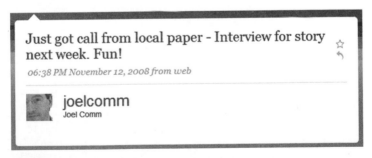

Figure 8.10 News about Joel Comm.
Who cares about my interview? Well, I do, and by showing that I'm excited about it, I hope my followers get excited too ... and feel that if my local newspaper considers my work important enough to follow, it's important enough for them to follow too.

so that it sounds like it's coming from a real person, not from a company.

CUSTOMER SUPPORT

Customer support on Twitter is often seen by companies as the only reason to use the site. Once they have someone Twittering away and answering questions, they feel that they've done their job and that there's nothing else to do.

That's a big mistake.

It's not just a mistake because doing it badly—like BestBuy—can actually put people off. It's a mistake because good customer service itself can be good branding.

It shows that the company is available to anyone who needs their help and that it listens too.

Figure 8.11 Sarah from The Home Depot's corporate communications department shows off the company's customer service.

The Home Depot (twitter.com/thehomedepot) does this very, very well. Its tweets offer short seasonal tips to keep people reading but its real strength is the quality of its customer support. Even though one Twitter account can only address a fraction of the questions the company's customers are going to have, the impression it creates is that followers will find even better help at the store itself.

That's exactly what branding should do: make potential customers feel that the real thing is even better.

Include great customer service tweets in your timeline—tweets that address problems and tell people exactly where they can find solutions—and you'll add one important characteristic to your branding story.

FEEDBACK

Feedback tweets are similar to customer service tweets, but with an important difference. Customer service tweets are likely to be initiated by the customer. Instead of sitting on a phone line for half an hour wondering whether they should press 1, press the pound key, or hurl the phone at the wall, a customer can send a quick direct message to a company rep on Twitter and receive a response.

The customer gets the answer he or she needs almost right away. The company gets to help one customer and show lots of other customers that it's helpful, friendly, and keen to lend a hand.

But not all customer service comments are sent as direct messages or even as replies to tweets on the company's own timeline. Often they're just comments—usually rants—on their own timeline.

A company looking to use Twitter for branding can spot those tweets through alerts and react to them in the hope that it can stop negative publicity from spreading.

That's not always possible, but it does show that the company cares and that even if it's not perfect, it is trying to improve. That can be an important part of a brand image too.

Feedback, though, isn't just about listening to what people are saying about your company. It can also mean inviting people to say something about your company.

Starbucks has a second Twitter account (twitter.com/my starbucksidea) that supports its My Starbucks Idea Web site

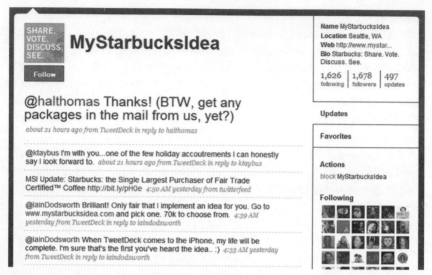

Figure 8.12 MyStarbucksIdea gives customers feedback and shows that the coffee chain is listening.

(mystarbucksidea.force.com). The site lets customers send in their proposals to improve the company and see how they're implemented.

The Twitter timeline allows the company to thank the customers for their ideas and explain what's happening to them.

It's a great way for the company to show that it sees itself as just one part of the Starbucks community—even if it doesn't produce immediate, direct sales.

SPECIAL OFFERS

Special offers are standard marketing practice and, as we've seen, can work on Twitter as well as anywhere else. Reward followers for reading your tweets by giving them exclusive deals that they feel they can't get anywhere else, and you'll give them an incentive to keep reading.

You'll also give yourself some extra sales.

Even an online publisher could do this by mentioning a great deal being offered by one of its affiliates. Include either your affiliate link in the code or link back to your Web page, and you could well generate some useful commissions.

Companies using Twitter for branding, though, have to be a little careful with the way they use special offers.

While discounts can be a very powerful way to drive customers to take immediate action, branding doesn't demand action. It simply requires the follower to keep reading and to think about the company in a certain way.

If you make lots of special offers, your customers won't be thinking about the company as a trusted friend that always delivers quality goods and services—they'll see it as a corporation keen to push its products.

Those special offers start to look like a hard sale, and hard selling doesn't work on Twitter.

If you want to make immediate, direct sales through Twitter, then regular special offers could be very effective. If you want to use the site to build a brand and create a community around your firm, then special offers should be scattered throughout your timeline just to reward your followers and keep them interested.

There's no golden rule about how many promotions is too many. It all depends on what else you're saying and who's following you. If you're making offers more frequently than one in five tweets, though, you're probably doing it too often.

Carnival Cruises (twitter.com/carnivalcruise) uses a range of social media strategies to promote its business and was a Twitter early adopter. It makes occasional special offers in its timeline.

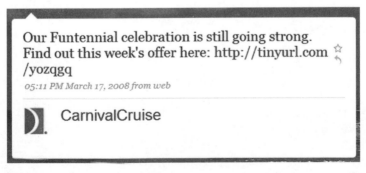

Figure 8.13   Carnival Cruise

Reinforce the Core Message

All of these tweets should look fairly familiar. There's a good chance that you're writing them anyway as you use Twitter to drive customers to take action.

But there's one type of tweet I haven't mentioned.

It's the one that the site was really created for, and one that I use frequently on my timeline: random thoughts.

People write all sorts of strange things on Twitter. It's one of the service's attractions. It's as though people have put a window on the side of their head and are letting the rest of us peek in every now and then to see what thoughts are passing through.

Yes, it's a bit nosey, and it shouldn't be very interesting—but it really is!

Tweets like these might be fun, but they aren't actionable. Tell your followers that one of your affiliates is running a special offer and include the link to your site, and you can expect people to click through.

Break news about a blog post that you've just put up, and you can expect people to come and read it.

Write a tweet that tells people that you're thinking of eating a donut and to heck with the calories, and the best you can hope is that they'll smile . . . and feel closer to you.

That's the benefit of these sorts of tweets: they create a better relationship with your followers, your customers, and your community.

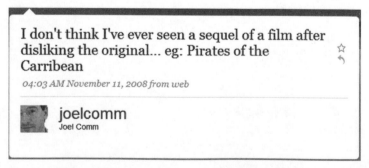

Figure 8.14   One of my random thoughts. They help with my brand image but would they help a company? I doubt it...

You're not just the owner of a Web site or some blogger on the Internet a million miles away. You're a real human being who thinks, works, and feels guilty about eating donuts. That sort of feeling can do wonders for the connection you have with your customers and with your readers. But I'm not sure that it will help with corporate branding.

A company's tweets should appear human, but they're not about the Twitterer; they're about the company. Adding what the Twitterer thinks about a piece of news he's broadcasting or an answer to a customer's question shows that the company really does care. Mention that the Twitterer fancies pizza, and the firm starts to look a little strange.

That isn't to say that random thoughts can play no part in branding on Twitter.

They do play a role, *but only in personal branding*.

I use them in my timeline because they help to brand me as a regular guy. That's important because I don't want other entrepreneurs to feel that Internet marketing is only for people with tons of marketing experience or who know how to program or who understand everything there is to know about the Internet. The fact that anyone can do it—even a family-focused, game-playing, non-coder like me—is an important part of the story I want to put across.

The same may be true when the Twitterer embodies the company. Tony Hsieh, for example, is the CEO of Zappos, an online retail store. He tweets on behalf of his company at twitter.com/zappos. Because this is his personal Twitter timeline, there's nothing wrong with Tony including random thoughts in his tweets—his tweets are first about him, not his company.

But because he's also the CEO of Zappos, something his background image makes clear, what he says also reflects the company.

This isn't exactly the same as branding. Tony Hsieh's tweets provide publicity for his company and build a community out of his customers. But beyond indicating that his company is open and approachable, they say little else about the firm.

By personalizing his tweets in this way, Tony turns his timeline into a branding tool that reinforces his image as the CEO of Zappos. That can be effective too. British tycoon Richard Branson has made a fortune by portraying himself as the face of Virgin. He's become a celebrity, and every time he appears in the press, he's promoting his

Figure 8.15 Tony Hsieh, CEO of Zappos, builds himself a brand and promotes his company at the same time.

business. Twitter is doing the same thing in a smaller way for Tony Hsieh—it's allowing him to build a personal brand that promotes his firm.

This is all about sticking to the core message. Once you know what you want your brand to look like and what you want it to say, it's important to make sure that your tweets say only that and don't confuse the message.

If you're tweeting on behalf of a company, keep it human, but not too personal.

If you're tweeting on behalf of a personal brand, include the random thoughts, but reduce the offers.

Those simple guidelines should help to keep your tweets on message.

Repetition, Repetition, Repetition

To keep your tweets on message, though, you will have to repeat them.

One of the challenges of any branding campaign is that the effect is never long-lasting. That's why even companies like Coca-Cola have to keep spending millions of dollars every year to keep their products in the public eye.

When you're using Twitter for branding, you don't have to spend millions of dollars to keep your market's attention.

You just have to keep sending out tweets.

There are companies that make the mistake of starting a Twitter campaign to promote a particular product, drop Twitter when the campaign ends and then try to pick it up again months later. It's a strategy that can work—if you're not sending out tweets, you're not bothering anyone, so few followers will block your tweets. But you will lose momentum and your community can disappear.

When you're using Twitter as a branding tool, you need to be tweeting at least once a day, and ideally far more often than that.

That doesn't have to be as hard as it sounds.

Writing the Tweets

I admit, it does sound hard. I like tweeting. It's fun, it's interesting, it's enjoyable. I've had some great virtual conversations with some wonderful people, learned all sorts of fascinating things, and picked up information that I couldn't have learned any other way than on Twitter.

But it takes time, and when you're a busy executive using Twitter to promote your business rather than just tell the world what you had for breakfast, that time is an investment.

This is where the difference between a corporate tweet account and a private tweet account is important.

Zappo's CEO might be writing his own tweets, but not everyone does that. The tweets of big companies like Delta and Carnival Cruises aren't written by the corporations' CEOs. They're written by employees or public relations firms who have been given the job of promoting the company's brand on the Web.

You can do the exact same thing.

If you don't want to write your tweets yourself, hand over the job of creating your business's tweets to someone in your office. Let them be your company's Twitter presence. Give them the freedom to be human, and include their opinions as well as your company's.

And tell them to mix up each of the different kinds of tweets too.

You'll still get the familiarity with your followers that only Twitter can bring. But you'll do it without any effort, and your helper will probably enjoy it too.

Like any effective marketing channel, Twitter can be a valuable branding tool. It works as a personal branding tool, giving any individual an image that's memorable and recognizable, and it can function too as a corporate branding tool helping companies to stand out, win trust, and turn their customers into a community.

Even some of the world's biggest companies have recognized the power of Twitter to drive home their message, and while not all of them are doing it correctly, a number have come up with some valuable models that anyone can copy.

Branding brings long-term results. You can also use Twitter to create instant results. In the next chapter, I'm going to discuss some of the ways that you can drive behavior in your followers.

9

Leveraging the Power of Twitter to Drive Behavior in Your Followers

We've seen that there are all sorts of different ways of writing tweets on Twitter. And we've seen too that there all sorts of different uses to which you can put Twitter.

Probably the most common use to which marketers want to use Twitter, though, is to achieve immediate results. They see their followers as a pool of people who will one day give them money—either directly or with the help of advertising—and they want to write tweets that create those effects.

There's nothing wrong with that. It's a little shortsighted, but there's really nothing wrong with it.

You can certainly create tweets that drive your followers to take the steps that you want them to take. But you do have to be a little careful.

Your Twitter timeline is not a sales page. Gripping headlines and hard call-to-actions on Twitter are more likely to drive people away than drive them to buy. Your tweets need to be subtle. They have to build interest and trust. Only then will your followers feel that doing what you want them to do will be worth their while.

In this chapter—which may be the most important chapter in the book—I'm going to explain how to drive traffic to a Web site;

how to use surveys to gain data and build responses; and how to mine your customers for valuable feedback.

I'll then discuss how to build effective, action-oriented tweet strategies and, perhaps most important of all, how to keep track of the results.

Let's start by looking at the ways that you can drive followers to a Web site.

Driving Followers to a Web Site

We've already seen that it's possible on Twitter to include a URL in tweets. We've also seen that there are even systems available that can create these kinds of tweets automatically.

But that doesn't mean that anyone will click those links. Nor is it particularly useful if you want to send your followers to a site that isn't a blog.

Although driving traffic toward other content pages has to be one of the most common uses of Twitter, you might also want to send your followers to a purchase page, to a registration page, or to a page on which you hope they'll click an ad.

All of those are possible on Twitter.

Promoting a Blog on Twitter

When publishers first started writing blogs, they were meant to be nothing more than online diaries, a place for people to write their

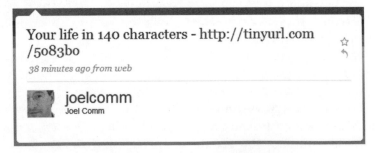

Figure 9.1 Headline and blog post URL make for an easy tweet and some helpful extra traffic. But is a headline enough to turn a follower into a reader?

thoughts and feelings and let anyone who wanted to read them do so.

They've become much more than that.

Today, blogs are a very effective publishing system. They've evolved to become online magazines, rather than personal pages.

The benefit is that publishers can now write about anything they want—and get paid for it too.

The disadvantage is that they're no longer personal.

If readers used to come to blogs to find what the writer was doing or thinking, today's blogs are often not even written by the bloggers themselves. Good, professional blogs tend to be filled with guest posts, paid writers, and ghostwriters. And there's nothing wrong with that.

The first thing that Twitter can do for a blog, then, is to bring back the personality of the publisher.

Bloggers can use Twitter to give readers a peek behind the scenes of their business, provide quick notices about their plans and the posts they're working on, and answer direct questions put to them by readers.

Sure, you can also do all of this on your blog—and ideally, you should.

But when your blog really takes off, it's unlikely that you'll have time to respond to every comment your posts receive. Articles about your blog are also likely to be less interesting to your readers than posts about cars, photography, or whatever it is that users are visiting your site to see.

Twitter can give publishers of blogs an alternative space to get closer to their readers, even when they're using content written by professional writers.

But what if you want to bring in new readers or increase the views of occasional visitors?

Twitter can help there too.

The principle is very simple. If you were to put an ad on AdWords to promote every blog post you publish, you'd have to pay a lot of money. Assuming you got the arbitrage right by weighing the cost of the ads against the revenue from the Web pages, you might make a small profit. But you'd need a lot of visitors to make it worthwhile.

Placing an announcement of a new blog post on Twitter is a very easy way to let lots of people know about it.

We've seen how Darren Rowse does this with his photography blog—a fantastic example of a highly successful blog that's much more of a magazine than a personal diary.

That's one very simple way to drive traffic from Twitter to a blog.

But that works because Darren Rowse's site is already well known. He doesn't have to do anything but remind his regular readers that a new post is online for those readers to stop by and take a look.

Darren's personal timeline is much more complex. His tweets contain a mixture of news announcements about his blogs as well as personal comments and answers to readers' questions.

That combination is important. Blog post headlines by themselves look very weak on Twitter. Even the sort of hard-hitting headline that social media types love (something like "20 Ways To Gain More Followers") can look desperate when it appears in a tweet.

Instead of saying something *about* you, they tell the reader that you really want them to be doing something *for* you: you want them to be reading your blog post.

That's exactly the wrong way to go about Twitter—and it's certainly the wrong way to go about driving followers to a blog post and encouraging them to become regular readers.

Twitter works best by creating curiosity. People read your tweets, become a part of your life and want to see what you're up to next. When you announce that you've just written a new blog post, they'll stop by to read it not just because the content is interesting, but because they're interested in what you wrote—or in what you published, if you didn't write it yourself.

Curiosity, though, doesn't come as a result of one tweet. It happens through publishing good tweets regularly.

When you first join Twitter, don't rush to fill your timeline with links that lead to your blog. Tweet about yourself, about what you're doing, thinking, and would like to be doing.

Reply to other people's tweets, especially those people who appear to have an interest in your topic—and in particular Twitterers with large followings, so that their replies to you will turn up in their timelines for everyone else to see.

Offer advice and solutions to Twitterers who have posed questions or are struggling with something in your field of expertise.

All of that will start to give you a core group of followers who are interested in who you are and what you can do for them. And so far, all you've done is help them. In effect, you will have been priming your market by handing out freebies in the form of free advice—a tested marketing strategy.

Now when you introduce your blog posts, you should find that many of your followers will click through to read them. They'll know that you deliver good advice and they'll be hungry for more.

You can then continue this strategy of providing regular updates of informative and entertaining tweets, dotted with links to your blog.

And if you've already started Twittering, it's never too late to begin this strategy! Just make sure that you add plenty of good tweets before you next post a link to your blog.

Priming your followers in this way should help to maximize your clickthroughs, but usually blogs, like Twitter, are a means to an end.

The end result that most publishers want is for their readers to click an ad or make a purchase. With a little thought, you can use Twitter to increase the chances that that will happen, too.

This takes a little skill and some planning. You have to know what sort of ads are likely to appear on your blog page, and you have to prepare your followers for them on Twitter.

That's unlikely to happen with your AdSense units. I'm a big fan of AdSense, and you should definitely be using it on your Web site, but because the ads can change so unexpectedly, you can't create interest in a particular product so that your readers are more likely to click an ad for it. You can only create top-quality content and optimize the units so that readers click the ads to find out more.

Curiosity is a powerful driving factor on blogs, too.

But AdSense isn't the only way you can put ads on a blog, and therefore it's not the only way you can monetize your Twitter followers.

You should certainly be including some cost-per-mile ads that pay for every view you receive. That will give you some money for every follower who clicks through, even if the individual amounts are small.

More important, though, is that you load up on affiliate ads. These are predictable—you choose the products—and unlike the products promoted in AdSense units, you can recommend these yourself.

Do you see how this creates a golden opportunity in Twitter?

Imagine that you ran a blog about video games. You could create a series of tweets about the game.

The first tweet could say that you're going to buy it.

The second tweet could say that the graphics have blown you away and that it looks like a killer game.

The third tweet could say that you've discovered a bunch of fantastic strategies and that the game is even better than you expected.

And the fourth tweet would include the URL of a blog post that offered a complete review of the game or tips to complete it. Included on the Web page would an affiliate ad from Amazon that led directly to the game.

You can add these affiliate links very easily by signing up as an Amazon Associate (the site's term for affiliates). You'll be able to choose the product you want to promote and paste the code onto your Web page. Every time someone clicks on that ad, you get a share of the revenue.

You'd need to run a tweet series like this fairly quickly. You want people to buy from your site; you don't want them to get excited and buy directly from Amazon, cutting you out of the loop. To keep your most ardent followers waiting for you—and for everyone else to catch up—you could point out that your blog will soon be running a review. That should give them a reason to put off their decision to buy until they've read what you have to say . . . and seen your ad.

The result should be that Twitter gives you the chance to create a kind of teaser campaign that can give you affiliate earnings when you launch your blog post.

Twitter as a Resource for Post Ideas

So with the right combination of tweets, you can use Twitter to drive followers to a page with a targeted ad. But you can also use your followers for a second purpose, and one that's no less valuable.

You can use them as a resource for blog post ideas.

Ask your followers what sort of posts they'd like to see on your blog and you're likely to get swamped with ideas.

That makes life very easy for you.

At the beginning of every month, you could just ask your followers what issues they'd like to see covered on your blog in the next few weeks.

No more beating your head against the wall trying to think up new content. And no more wondering if people are going to like the concept, either.

Before you write about a particular subject, you could just ask your followers what they think. If everyone says it sounds a bit dull or asks how you're going to deal with this aspect or approach that problem you haven't even considered, you can start thinking again. You won't have to wait until you've been sweating over the post for a couple of hours to discover it isn't going to work.

And of course once you've written it, you can be sure that when you announce that it's online you'll have an audience for it.

This can be fascinating stuff. Mine your followers for information and you'll be amazed at the responses you get. More importantly, asking a crowd for ideas will help to keep your blog fresh and ticking over, an important consideration when you've been doing it for a while and you've already covered all the information that you think important . , , several times.

Fatigue is one of the biggest dangers for a mature blog, but by giving you a giant bank of editorial advisors to call on, Twitter can help your blog stay young and fresh.

There are a couple of ways you can mine this kind of information.

The first is to ask a straightforward, open-ended question. A tweet that says: "What would you like to see covered on the blog this month?" could get you a ton of interesting answers.

A tweet that said, "Want to guest post on my blog? Send me a DM." would land you a ton of interesting content.

But you do have to be careful here. Your blog is successful because *you* create it. You came up with the subject, you set the topics for the posts and for the most part, you're likely to be writing it. Hand over too much influence to your readers—or followers—and there's a risk that you'll dilute the characteristics that have made your site so interesting.

While readers might say they want posts about this subject or content about that topic, they're often the worst judges of what they really need—and they certainly want to be surprised by excellent content that they hadn't thought of themselves.

That's why a good alternative option is to give your followers a choice. Instead of asking them what content they'd like to see, offer them three subjects and ask which they'd like to see most. That will give you a good idea of your followers' preferences—and if you get a close call, you can still write about all of them.

Announcing your new blog posts on Twitter can help to create a few more views and win you some extra revenue. Using your followers as a resource for post ideas can help to keep your blog focused and informative. And of course, the people who see tweets about your blog posts won't be restricted to your followers. Although your followers are likely to give you the highest number of clickthroughs, plenty of people will also click through your timeline without following you. They'll see your blog links and your supporting tweets too, and many of them will visit your blog as a result.

Those extra clicks, both from dedicated followers interested in you and your topic and from curious passersby, are important reasons for marketing a blog on Twitter. It's why blog promotion is one of the main uses of Twitter, even if that use is often restricted to automated Twitterfeeds.

But Twitter can do a lot more than drive followers to a blog page.

It can also drive them to buy.

Driving Followers to the Mall

Look through my timeline and you'll see lots of different kinds of tweets. You'll see links to my blog posts. You'll see replies to my followers. You'll see my opinions on politics, gaming, and social media. You'll even see the odd quote that I've thrown in for fun and to spark some comments.

What you won't see are tweets that tell people they should be buying my products.

That's not why I use Twitter. I prefer to use it to build a brand and a community. In time, that will bring me more loyal customers and more sales overall. I can already see it happening in the number of visitors to my blog and the type of comments those visitors make.

But that doesn't mean you can't use Twitter to drive direct sales. You can, but you have to follow a number of simple rules:

♦ *Don't do it too often*.

A special offer once a week is plenty. More than that and you'll start to look like a commercial Twitter timeline, rather than a personal one. That will reduce the number of your users.

♦ *Make the offers really special*.

Time-limited offers and discount coupons make followers feel that they're being rewarded for reading your tweets. Being part of an exclusive club is a powerful motivator to keep reading.

♦ *Keep the offers targeted*.

People will follow you for all sorts of reasons. They might have seen your Twitter URL on your blog, they might have seen a reply to you in someone else's timeline, or they could have read one of your retweeted messages, to name just three.

And they'll stick around because they find your tweets interesting and entertaining.

With a group of followers that could be quite varied, the temptation might be to make offers for any products you can think of. If someone offers you an interesting-looking joint venture, you might want to mention it on Twitter, offer a discount code, and see if anyone bites.

You could do that. And some people might bite.

But if your keep your offers closely targeted to your specialized subject—whatever that subject might be—you'll continue to come across as an expert, and because your trust levels on that topic will be higher, your conversion rates should be higher too.

♦ *Don't link to a sales page without a special offer*.

Twitter is still in its early stages. Although Twitterers understand that companies are using the system for branding and marketing, they don't want to feel that they're being pushed into buying. If the tweets are interesting and entertaining, followers will be happy to read them.

In fact, they'll enjoy them and they'll see the company as having its finger on the pulse, as a firm that feels that it's part of their community and knows how to follow the community's rules.

Companies that are seen to view followers as nothing more than walking moneybags, though, aren't going to pick up followers. They're actually more likely to lose followers who were once customers.

Link directly to a sales page without making the follower feel that they're receiving special treatment, and you create the impression that you really want to sell, not tweet.

Usually, the best way to drive followers to buying pages then is to use the strategies we've seen already: create entertaining tweets and throw in occasional special offers that appear to reward followers while avoiding the appearance of a hard sale—or even the appearance that you're marketing.

There is one exception, though. A number of timelines have turned up on Twitter that take exactly the opposite approach. They're a bit like Darren Rowse's Twitterfeed account: they provide just one type of tweet and followers know exactly what they're getting.

In this case, they're getting nothing but special offers.

Timelines like these have the potential to be good revenue generators. Building up followers will be a challenge, though. Because a Twitterer running a timeline like this is rarely going to be interacting with other Twitterers, it will be harder than usual to pick up momentum and build a big follower list.

You could tap the users of your Web site, which will turn the timeline into a kind of RSS feed that reminds your regular readers that you have new content.

Or you could set up a separate timeline with a mixture of different kinds of tweets, like Darren Rowse has done, and retweet occasionally from your sales timeline to share the followers.

Figure 9.2 Once in a while MomsWhoSave (twitter.com/ momswhosave) will toss in a personal tweet. But it's mostly discounts and coupon codes for its 694 followers.

And of course, each time you send out an e-mail burst of coupons, you could make sure that it includes your Twitter URL to turn your list into followers.

Above all though, you're going to need a regular supply of great offers!

Can You Put Affiliate Links on Twitter?

It's just so tempting. You've spotted a great product, you've got an affiliate code that could land you piles of cash if you can persuade people to buy, and you've got a long follower list made up of people who could really benefit from the product.

So all you have to do is toss a short version of the link into one of your tweets, and hey presto—piles of cash. Right?

Actually, yes.

Well, okay, there's a little more to it than that.

Just like any item you're hoping to sell through Twitter, affiliate products have to be well targeted to suit your followers. The people who read your tweets should be able to see that you're genuinely interested in benefiting them rather than in benefiting yourself.

Figure 9.3   Internet entrepreneur Jamie Holt (twitter.com/
jayxtreme) scatters some affiliate links throughout his timeline.

Like affiliate links anywhere, you'll always do better when you recommend the products you're linking to, rather than just throwing them at your readers cold.

And like any marketing push on Twitter, try not to do it too often and make sure that you include plenty of other kinds of tweets to soften the marketing effect and increase the feeling that you're recommending a chance find.

If you're in any doubt—or if you find that start to lose followers after including affiliate links in your timeline—you can always place the link on a Web page and promote that page instead.

Driving Followers to Register

So you can use Twitter to build a brand, and you can use Twitter to drive followers to buy right away, too.

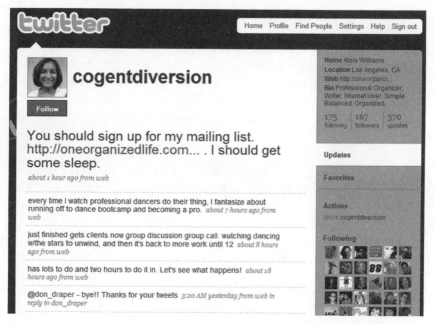

Figure 9.4   Alaia Williams (twitter.com/cogentdiversion) makes a not-very-subtle request for subscribers. Notice how she adds a comment to it as well, though, so that it doesn't look like spam.

But there are even more things that you can do with Twitter and, with the right tweets, persuade your followers to do.

One action that's become very popular with bloggers, for example, is persuading readers to sign up for their RSS feeds. By itself, that doesn't generate revenue. But it does mean that readers are more likely to return, less likely to miss posts, and more likely to click ads or make a purchase one day.

On the one hand, persuading followers to do this is very simple. If your followers enjoy your tweets and if they're clicking through the links to your blog post, then they're likely to be keen to read more. Sending a tweet pointing out that they can sign up for your RSS feed should be enough to persuade many of them to click through and hand over their e-mail addresses.

That's particularly true when you make those invitation tweets look like opportunities for the follower, rather than a benefit for you.

When Alaia Williams, a professional organizer and blogger, suggested that her followers should sign up for her mailing list, she softened the request by adding that she should get some sleep.

That was a nice way of signing off for the night that also told her followers how they can continue reading even while she's not available.

Any Twitterer could follow that example by tweeting something like:

"That's all for now, I'm off to watch telly. You can read more at http://tinyurl.com/afsfhi and don't forget to join the mailing list."

Do you see how a tweet like that doesn't just recommend that your followers sign up, but leaves them somewhere to go to continue reading your content?

If you can frame your recommendations in a way that looks like you're helping your followers—rather than trying to get them to help you—you'll always get better results.

Tracking Results and Testing Strategies

The success that I've enjoyed at Internet marketing didn't come about through good luck.

I'd like to say that it happened because I'm incredibly talented and interesting—but no. I can't say that either. Not honestly anyway.

Sure, the content I was putting up on my sites was good. It had to be good, otherwise no one would read it, no matter how well I marketed the site. Reading my site was interesting—at least my users thought so. But there was a part that was quite boring.

I would keep a diary that described exactly what each ad unit looked like, where it was located on the page and what kind of ads it was offering. Next to that description, I would write exactly how many views those ads received, how many clickthroughs, and how much money the page generated.

Then I would change the color or the placement or a few keywords and track the result of the change for a week.

It was painstaking stuff and strangely a lot more interesting than it sounds. But within a few months I understood what kind of ad formats generated the most clickthroughs, in which locations, and with what sort of content. I also knew which subjects gave me the highest-earning keywords.

It was a huge breakthrough, and it meant that I could target my content and my ad space to bring in maximum revenues. Every time I made a change or put up a new Web page, I knew what the result would be.

It didn't give me complete control over all the moneymaking aspects of my Web site, because traffic flows and Google, like the weather, can be unpredictable. But I think I got as close as it's possible to get—and I certainly got to enjoy the rewards.

I was able to collect that data because AdSense supplies some pretty detailed stats. What Google wasn't telling me, I could pick up from my server logs. With some quick calculations, it became pretty easy to test, track, and record.

It's no surprise, then, that I'm a huge fan of testing on Internet marketing. It's the only way keep control of your site and avoid wasting time and money on experiments that don't pay off. If you're not earning all the income you think you should be, you can spot the problem quickly and correct it. It takes a little while, but once you understand exactly what makes your site tick—and the money flow through—you should have no problem at all keeping it profitable.

The same principle is true on Twitter, but there *is* a problem . . . Twitter doesn't provide detailed stats.

The only figures that Twitter will tell you are how many people you're following, how many people are following you, and how many updates you've posted.

That's useful as far as it goes—but it really doesn't go very far.

Testing and tracking on Twitter, then, will involve looking at your Twitter stats, your timeline, and your alerts.

But it's also going to involve looking at your server logs to follow the results.

Twitter alone will be able to tell you:

♦ Which kinds of tweets generate the most replies

♦ Which kinds of tweets get the most retweets

♦ Which replies from which other Twitterers bring you the most followers

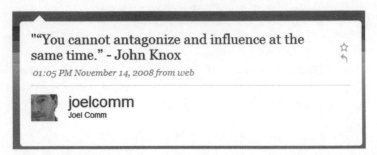

Figure 9.5   What does this quote do, I wonder . . .

To gather this data, you would need to test different versions of each kind of tweet. Let's say, for example, that you had tweeted something that had little to do with your business but which you thought your followers might find interesting, such as an inspiring quote.

You post the tweet, record it in your Twitter Journal, and wait a day to see how many replies and retweets that tweet receives.

Now, a day on Twitter can be a long time. On a blog, it usually takes a week to see how a different ad placement or a post on a particular topic affects your revenue, but on Twitter, you have to move much faster than that. A day is plenty of time to deliver the data you need.

It *is* possible to post other tweets in the meantime, but when you're testing, I don't recommend it. Followers are more likely to comment on the newer posts than the older ones, so you'd skew the results. You might want to set aside one day each week for testing, but change the day regularly so that your followers feel that they should be looking out for your tweets every single day.

Let's say then that out of 200 followers, your inspirational quote generates 12 replies, and you can see from the alerts you set up for your Twitter username that it also picked up four retweets. The following week, you might want to try it again with a different quote to see if you get a different result, but let's say you see similar figures.

You also find that while your follower list has been growing at an average of say, 10 followers per week, the weeks in which you include an inspirational quote give you 13 followers.

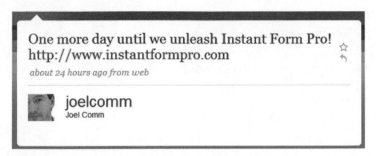

Figure 9.6 And what does this tweet do?

So now you can say that tweeting inspiration quotes gives you around twelve replies, four retweets and three additional followers.

That's valuable information. Now you can compare it to a different kind of tweet. This time you post a tweet that alerts your followers to a new product you're launching.

Again, you'll want to:

♦ Record the tweet in your journal

♦ Count the number of replies you receive

♦ Note who replied, so that you know which of your followers are most likely to respond to your tweets

♦ Track how often the post is mentioned and retweeted based on your username alerts

♦ Add up the number of new followers you receive in the hours following the post

That will tell you the effect the tweet has had on your Twitter account. But when you're including a link, you'll also want to know how many people are clicking through. You can discover this from your server logs and possibly from your URL-shortening service, depending on which one you're using.

You might find, then, that a tweet with a link to a product gives you six replies (including four from regulars), three retweets and three new followers.

You might also find that according to your server log you got eight clickthroughs from Twitter . . . and made two sales.

Now you know that a tweet like that is worth three new followers, a four-percent clickthrough rate . . . *and $60*, if the product costs $30.

So all you have to do is keep sending out tweets like this and you'll make $60 each time, right?

It's not that easy.

Tracking Multiple Tweets

If you remember just one piece of information from this book, make it this:

Tweeting is a process.

Write a blog post and you can see the results right away. You'll be able to count the views, check the clickthroughs, and calculate the value of a post on that topic.

Most importantly, those figures are relatively consistent.

Although there's no such thing as complete predictability on the Internet, each time you put up a blog post that covers the topic and is optimized in the same way, you should see roughly similar results.

The same isn't true on Twitter.

Discover that a certain kind of tweet gets your followers clicking through to your Web site and persuades a few of them to buy or click ads, and you might be tempted to do it again a few hours later.

This time though, instead of picking up three new followers and earning $60 in sales, you get no new followers, one clickthrough and no sales.

What went wrong?

Not the tweet with the link—you've already seen that tweets like these can work.

It was the tweets that came before the link tweet.

Followers don't want to receive the same content all the time on Twitter. And they're not going to click every link you offer them.

If you want to increase the odds that your followers click a link that you offer them on Twitter, make the sure that the previous tweets *don't* contain links.

They won't be suffering from click fatigue, and, because linking isn't something you do too often, the link will appear to be more valuable.

So if you wanted to post a tweet that drove your followers to a Web site where you were selling a new e-book or that included a valuable affiliate link, you'd want to prepare the ground with five or six tweets that offer interesting content or that let people know that the product is in preparation.

How will you know which kind of content to include?

By looking back at your timeline.

Looking at your timeline will tell you which tweet sequences you've used in the past in the build up to the link tweet. By comparing those sequences with differences in the clickthroughs and conversions from those link tweets, you should be able to see which sequence of tweets is likely to be the most effective.

Let's see how this might work in practice.

Imagine that you're the publisher of a blog about gardening. You use Twitter to build a community of readers, answer questions about gardening issues, mine your followers for knowledge about sourcing seeds and cuttings, and, of course, to send them to your blog posts.

You then make an agreement with the author of an e-book on managing a small garden, but before you put up a tweet containing a link to the sales page and urging people to check out a great book, you want to make sure that you get as many clickthroughs as possible.

So you look back over your Twitter Journal to see which of the tweets you've posted in the past that contain links generated the largest number of clickthroughs.

You find that tweet in your timeline, and as well as checking what you wrote in that tweet, you also examine what you wrote in the five or six tweets that came before it.

Let's say that those tweets were:

"First daffodil of the spring bloomed yesterday. What a sight!"

"Thinking of replanting my bonsai. Anyone know which store has the best selection of pots?"

"Putting down a new layer of mulch. Whiffy stuff."

"Spraying the bougainvillea. I wish it wasn't so big and thorny."

"A beautiful spring day—warm, sunny and with just a few clouds. Let's keep the rain off for a few days."

You could then categorize those tweets as:

Random thought.

Question.

Action.

Action.

Random thought.

And to increase the chances that your link to the e-book affiliate link would generate at least an equal number of clickthroughs, you could repeat the sequence before you posted that tweet:

"I love walking around my garden in the evening. It's so quiet and colorful!"

"Apple tree is starting to blossom. Anyone know whether the bee population recovered this year?"

"Looking at designs for small gardens. So many wonderful new possibilities."

"Thinking about laying a new garden path."

"Small gardens can look so beautiful . . . when they're well planned."

"John Smith has written a wonderful book about miniature gardening. Check it out at http://tinyurl.com/bihiyi."

Is it possible that a different sequence of tweets would have produced more clickthroughs? Of course, but when you're Twittering for money, it's a good idea to play it safe—and besides, unless you're tracking the results of your tweets, you won't know which sequence!

One of the most enjoyable aspects of using Twitter is that you can do it spontaneously. Maintaining a blog requires thought and planning. The posts themselves take time to research and write, but Twitter is something you can use whenever you feel like it.

That ease of use is part of what makes Twitter so much fun.

Even when you're testing and tracking, in the way I've described in this chapter, you can still tweet spontaneously. There's nothing wrong with continuing to post individual tweets as well as tweet sequences.

Nor do you have to record the results of all your tweets. A representative sample should be enough let you understand what different tweets and sequences do.

Tracking can take time, and it demands a little attention. But it can churn up some fascinating information, and it means that you can maximize the chances that a tweet will have exactly the effect you want.

Making the Most of Twitter's Trends

So far I've been talking about the statistics you can pick up about your own tweets. But there's another kind of data that you can pick up on Twitter.

Figure 9.7 Flaptor's Twist tells you exactly what's hot on Twitter . . . and when!

You can see what topics other people are discussing.

Twitter provides some information about trends. Head to the search page and you can see a list of ten "trending topics." Much more detailed—and far more interesting—is the information provided by search company Flaptor's Twist program (twist.flaptor.com).

The site looks a little like Alexa and offers a graph showing the number of times a chosen topic has turned up in tweets over a period of time. You can enter more than one topic to compare the most popular terms and you can zoom in to see the stats for a chosen time.

You can even see sample tweets containing the terms in your search.

The right of the screen shows the current 10 most popular topics and another 10 topics that were recently popular.

It's all fascinating stuff, and you can have a lot of fun tossing in keywords to find out whether "Mac" is more popular than "PC," "trees" more popular than "flowers," and so on.

But the information you find on Twist can be valuable too. *It lets you attract lots of followers by tweeting about popular topics, and it means you can tap a known market.*

There are limitations here, of course. Stray too far from the usual subject of your tweets and you'll struggle to turn readers into followers and you'll struggle even harder to keep them as followers.

But if you can combine your usual topic with a popular subject —and offer good, unique content—you'll have a passport to the largest discussions currently taking place on Twitter.

Let's say, for example, that you're a gardening Twitterer and you wanted to build up your follower list quickly so that you can get as many people as possible clicking your link.

You look on Twist and see that the most popular topic currently being discussed on the site is "Gmail" and the second most popular is "themes." You can't find any reasonable way to link gardening with Gmail, but you could enter a discussion about themes by asking what kind of flower themes people might like to see.

A search for the term on Twitter's search engine shows that the themes that people are discussing are, not surprisingly, Gmail's themes. It also shows who's discussing them.

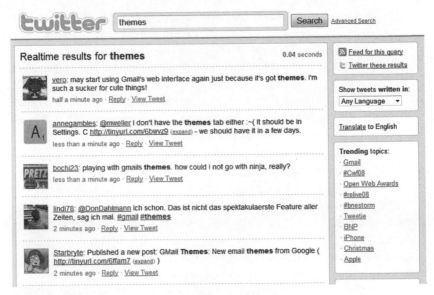

Figure 9.8   So who's talking about themes then?

What it won't show, unfortunately, is how many followers those people have. You'll only be able to tell that by clicking through to their tweets until you find someone with a good number of readers—a number in the hundreds should be enough—and ideally, a few tweets about gardening too.

You follow them, then reply to their tweet about themes with a tweet of your own:

"These themes are cool. Do you know if it's possible to edit them? I'd love to use a pic of my garden."

When that Twitterer replies, it should bring a few of their followers clicking through to your Twitter page. And because it's a hot topic, *if your tweet is a genuinely valuable contribution*, there's also a good chance that the discussion will spread to other Twitter pages too, giving you even more followers.

Make this follower-building strategy part of your preparation for an important link tweet, and you'll be able to make the most of a Twitter campaign.

Twitter works in all sorts of wonderful ways. Usually, it works as a fun way for people to keep in touch with others, make new friends, and join discussions. That's how most people use it.

It also works as a tool for mining information and finding expert advice.

And plenty of smart companies are using it to build a brand, turn their customers into a community, and cement the name of their products in the minds of their market.

But it's also possible to use Twitter to prompt people to take a particular course of action.

In this chapter, we've seen how it's possible to use tweets to send people to a blog, to persuade them to buy, and to add them to your e-mail list.

And we've seen to how tracking your results and your tweets—and trends too—can help you to get the most out of the actions you want your followers to take.

All of that comes from using Twitter as you find it on the Web. Twitter, though, extends beyond the Web. In the next chapter, we'll look at some of the tools that make Twitter even more useful.

10

Beyond Twitter.com

Third-Party Tools You Will Want to Know

One of the things that really makes Twitter fun is that it comes with lots of optional add-ons. Twitter allows programmers to write applications that anyone can use and that extend the power of the service.

Some of them are a little odd. (I've yet to find a good use for Twitter in Second Life.) But some of them are extremely helpful. For example, there are all sorts of applications that let you send and follow tweets without opening your browser.

That makes for hours of exciting experimentation—just the sort of thing that tech-minded people love to do.

On the other hand, if you want to skip straight to the most useful apps, here are some that I recommend.

TweetLater

Follow someone on Twitter and there's a good chance that they'll follow you in return. It's not guaranteed, but it does happen a lot and it's why one strategy to pick up followers is to do a lot of following.

The reason it happens a lot is that reciprocal following looks like good manners. If someone's following you, then it only seems right you should follow them back. As we've seen, that might not be the smartest move—it can make you look like a spammer, and

187

Figure 10.1   TweetLater lets you schedule your tweets in advance.

you can't possibly follow everyone on a long list closely—but many people do it anyway.

And one reason they do it is that it's easy. TweetLater (www.tweetlater.com) lets you set up autofollows. Whenever someone follows you, you'll automatically follow them in return.

That can be a pretty neat trick but it's not the service's main function.

The biggest reason for using TweetLater is that it lets you set up tweets in advance—a bit like an autoresponder.

Now that really can be valuable.

It means that you can keep your timeline ticking over even while you're sleeping, working your day job, or spending the weekend with the kids. You wouldn't want to create a false impression on your timeline by preparing tweets that say you're hard at work on a blog post while in fact you're relaxing at a spa, but you can prepare some random thoughts and other tweets to keep your timeline active.

Best of all, you can use TweetLater to prepare a series of tweets that lead up to a link you want your followers to click through.

TweetLater also provides keyword alerts, which can be useful, and automatic "thank you's" to followers, which you need to use carefully. Fill your timeline with personal thank you's and your tweets look dull for everyone else. TweetLater recommends sending your welcome messages by direct message, and I think that's a good idea. You can save the reward of a mention in your timeline for people who reply to your tweets.

TweetLater is free and available at www.tweetlater.com, but you might also want to check out Twittertise (www.twittertise.com). This does almost exactly the same thing, but also lets you see the number of clickthroughs on links that you insert into the tweet.

Twitterific

Twitter might have been designed with mobiles in mind, but it was never very mobile-friendly.

Fortunately, developers have come up with some pretty cool alternatives.

Twitterific is a Twitter client that sits on a Mac's desktop. It shows tweets from your followers and lets you tweet back in return. The interface is attractive and fun, and the program means you don't have to work with your Twitter page open in your browser.

Figure 10.2   Twitterific

Best of all, Twitterific is also available for the iPhone. It even comes with a minibrowser so that you don't lose your timeline every time you click a link, and it lets followers see where you are.

It's a very neat solution for Twitterers on the move. Twitterific is available for download from Icon Factory at http://iconfactory.com/software/twitterrific. The free version is funded by ads, but you can get an ad-free version for $14.95.

Twhirl

Twitterific is very cool and a neat solution for iPhone users (and Tweetie, available from the iPhone app store, is great too). Owners of other types of mobile phones can try TwitterMail (www.twittermail.com) for e-mail–enabled phones; Cellity (www.cellity.com) for Java-enabled phones; and TwitterBerry (www.orangatame.com/products/twitterberry/) for BlackBerry phones.

For desktop Twitterers, Twitterific is also limited: it only works on the Mac. PC users have to look elsewhere for a Twitter client. Many of them look to Seesmic's Twhirl.

Like Twitterific, Twhirl frees Twitterers from Twitter's Web page, letting them send and receive tweets from an attractive, instant message-style client. It's packed with all sorts of other useful

Figure 10.3   Twhirl

> **Thanks to your nominations, twitterfeed has made it into the OWA shortlist - now vote for us!** (You can vote once a day until 30th Nov.)
>
> SHARE
> not logged in [login/register] | help | blog
>
> *... feed your blog to twitter*
>
> **Getting started**
> Here's how to get your blog (or any other RSS or Atom feed) twittering:
>
> 1. Create a new twitter user at twitter.com (or use your existing one)
>
>   this twitter user is going to be the one posting your blog entries - twitterfeed needs to know your chosen twitter username and password so it can post your blog updates to your twitter account
>
> 2. Login to twitterfeed using your OpenID
>
>   OpenID is a standard for providing single sign on between web sites
>   You can register your own OpenID for free, or may even be able to use your existing blog ID [more]
>
> 3. Provide us with the URL for your blog's RSS feed, and how often we should post to twitter

Figure 10.4 Twitterfeed

goodies too, such as automatic short URLs, search, and image posting to TwitPic. It's built on Adobe AIR, so you'll have to download that first, but both are free and available from www.twhirl.org.

Twitterfeed

I've mentioned Twitterfeed a few times in this book. Spend any time at all reading tweets and you're going to come across plenty of examples of its use.

As a way of adding one particular type of content to your timeline, Twitterfeed can be very useful. But do bear in mind that the price you're paying for the ease of providing blog updates through Twitter is a loss of the personal touch. If your blog is hugely popular, you can get away with a Twitterfeed timeline dedicated solely to informing followers of your latest posts.

For most people, though, Twitterfeed's updates become just one kind of tweet—but one that they can set up and leave.

Sign up for free at twitterfeed.com.

Figure 10.5   Twist

Twist

There are a number of different services that allow Twitterers to keep track of the popularity of various topics and keywords on Twitter. Some use a frequently updated tag cloud to show relative popularity, but I like the graphs on Twist. It's accurate and detailed, you can make comparisons between different terms, and even see samples of the tweets you're examining.

It can be a very useful way to make sure that you're targeting the most popular terms and look for other people Twittering about your topic.

And it looks very neat too.

Use it at twist.flaptor.com.

Twellow

Twist can help you find people with similar interests to your own but Twellow makes it all much, much easier. Run by WebProNews, it's supposed to be a kind of Yellow Pages of social media, but it operates more like a Twitter Yahoo!.

The site tracks conversations on Twitter and places the Twitterers behind them into various categories. Click one of those categories and you'll be able to see a list of suitable Twitterers,

Figure 10.6 Twellow

complete with sample tweet, bio, image, and the number of their followers.

For Twitterers looking for interesting and useful people to follow, it's a fantastic resource.

And clearly, for Twitterers who want to be followed, it's hugely valuable too.

Once you start sending tweets, you should find that you're added automatically, but if you can't find your name on the site, you can add it yourself. In any case, it's certainly worth checking the categories that you've been listed under and self-editing them if necessary.

Keep Twellow close by at www.twellow.com.

TweetBeep

Twellow tells you who tends to talk about what, but you'll also want to know who's talking about your topics now.

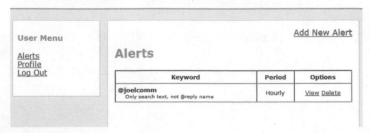

Figure 10.7   TweetBeep

TweetBeep, which as we've seen sends out regular alerts when-ever a keyword is used on Twitter, is really a must for anyone thinking about marketing through microblogging.

Remember that tracking your username or your company name and diving right into a conversation can look a little creepy. If you see someone has mentioned you, it's often a good idea to follow them before replying.

You can set up your alerts at tweetbeep.com.

TwitterCounter

There's one more useful matrix you might want to know when you're looking for people to follow—and when you want to know how you're doing, too—and that's the rate of follower growth.

When you're tracking your own tweets and their results, you should have those figures handy, but when you look at someone else's profile, there's no way of knowing whether they picked up all of their followers a year ago or whether their tweets are still generating interest.

TwitterCounter lets you see anyone's follower numbers over time.

Just toss a name into the site and you'll receive a graph showing how their follower numbers have risen and fallen over the last week.

Interesting, and when you're looking for people on the up to follow and be followed by, useful too.

Have fun at www.twittercounter.com.

Figure 10.8   TwitterCounter

TweetDeck

Twitter's strength is its simplicity. Short posts, short replies, and quick conversations make for a service that's simple to use. But it's also very limited. It's not easy to keep track of conversations, for example. You'll be holding multiple chats with multiple followers

Figure 10.9   TweetDeck

all at the same time and often on different topics. As one tweet comes in, the last one will pushed down the list, making it difficult to follow the course of an exchange.

Nor does Twitter allow you to group tweets and followers according to subject.

TweetDeck lets you do that.

This service really is a must-have for anyone with a large list of followers. You can create multiple columns and group them according to topics. It's the closest you're likely to get to Facebook's groups.

You'll need to download Adobe AIR again, but it's still free and available at www.tweetdeck.com.

TwitThis

TwitThis isn't exactly a Twitter application, but it's certainly useful nonetheless and should be a basic tool for any Twitter-based marketer.

You've probably seen all the buttons at the bottom of blog posts urging people to Digg the article or send it to StumbleUpon. With

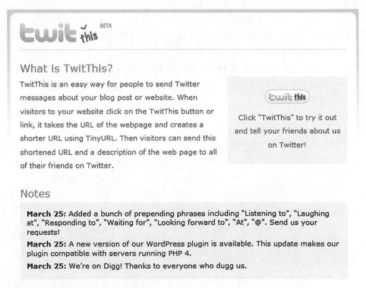

Figure 10.10   TwitThis

TwitThis, you can also ask them send a URL of the page together with a brief description to their Twitter followers.

It's a simple and effective way to help your blog or Web site make the most of Twitter's viral power.

Load up on your buttons at www.twitthis.com.

These are just 10 of the most useful tools that I've found for Twitter. There are plenty of others, and new ones are coming out every day with better interfaces, more features, and neater designs.

You can have hours of fun downloading them and trying them out until you create the toolkit that works best for you. Because many of them are fairly similar, much comes down to personal taste.

On the whole though, your toolkit should contain applications that let you find people to follow, track keywords, organize your followers, and tweet and reply easily. Those are the basics.

In addition, some companies have begun experimenting with using Twitter as an advertising channel. Magpie (www.be-a-magpie .com) inserts targeted ads into your timeline, and Twittad (www .twittad.com) allows Twitterers to turn their background images into advertising billboards onto which companies can place their own ads.

While both of these programs look interesting, both have problems. Twitterers who use Magpie have no control over the ads that appear, and it's not yet clear whether followers will accept ads in timelines. Twittad means losing what could be your most important branding tool, and with prices that range from $20 a week for a timeline with 259 followers to $45 for a timeline with more than 7,500 followers, you'll probably be better off putting your own links on the background.

TwitPwr.com

If you paste a long URL into a tweet, Twitter will automatically create a TinyURL to shorten it. However, there are many other sites that you can use to shorten your own URLS. TwitPwr.com not only shortens URLS, but also provides a unique Twitter tool that has viral appeal.

Not only are all clicks through your TwitPwr URLs tracked, but accounts are ranked to show their power. The premise is that true Twitter power is not to be judged by the number of followers,

Figure 10.11   TwitPwr.com

but rather by the influence the account holder has over the followers. One Twitterer may have 10,000 followers and 50 people follow a link he or she tweets. But another may have 1,000 followers and 75 people follow a tweeted link. Which is the more powerful Twitterer?

TwitPwr.com adds a unique twist to creating and tracking URLs that is sure to bring out competitive behavior in more than just a few Twitter users.

11

Building Powerful Solutions on Top of the Twitter Platform

So far we have talked about how to interact with Twitter in two primary ways: through the use of Twitter's own Web site and through the use of some excellent third-party applications that tie into the Twitter services. These two methods of interacting with Twitter are great and sufficient for most users, but they do lack one important feature if you are planning to take maximum advantage of the Twitter phenomenon—they require you to be at the computer and physically interacting with Twitter in a very manual way. This limits your Twitter experience to just what you can physically read, respond, and interact with via your keyboard and mouse.

I've often said that "I can't code my way out of a paper bag," and I believe it's true! That's why I've asked Ken Burge, the President of InfoMedia, Inc., to share his knowledge on integrating Twitter with your business from a technical perspective.

Having spent years at Texas Instruments and Microsoft, Ken has a keen understanding of technical issues. The rest of this chapter has been written by him.

In this chapter, I take the discussion one step further and show you how to monitor, participate in, and integrate Twitter into your own company's business systems so that your company can participate in the Twitter community in a way that yields maximum results through the use of automation, leverage, and a few simple tools Twitter makes available.

So why would you want to integrate Twitter into your company's information systems? The answer to that question goes right to the heart of why any business would want to use Twitter at all.

If you are holding true to the tenets of good business, then the only reason has to be to somehow improve the bottom line. Now this might be by taking a direct approach and trying to sell your wares directly to the Twitter community (generally frowned upon), or it might be a very indirect approach that takes the form of asking your customers for feedback or (following Comcast's lead) actively searching for disgruntled customers and offering them support. It is important to agree that both approaches (direct and indirect) have, at their heart, the goal of improving the company's bottom line in one way or another.

Now that we've agreed that a business's use of Twitter must have the motive of some kind of future profit, then we can begin to see where using some automated tools and methods would be beneficial. After all, it is the goal of any going concern to maximize shareholder value (or owner's profit), and that is most effectively done through the use of automation and leverage—not manual effort. It might help to define those two terms so that we are on the same page:

♦ *Automation*: The ability to take a manual process and put it on auto-pilot through the use of technology.

♦ *Leverage*: The ability to use a tool (in this case Twitter's automation features) to do more of something (in this case listen and respond to the market) than would otherwise be possible. Just as a lever allows you to move a much heavier object than would be otherwise possible, these techniques allow you to listen more, participate more, and help you reach your goal of increased profits for your company.

What Does Twitter Provide?

One thing that Twitter does very well is make its data available. In fact, there are so many ways to get access to the Twitter data that it can be confusing to know where to start. The easiest way to begin to explore the vast amount of data that is available inside Twitter is to use its own Search service.

Originally a third-party tool called summize.com, the search feature was acquired by Twitter in early 2008 and can be found by typing search.twitter.com into your browser. Once you arrive, you can type any search term into the search box, and the service will scan the Twitter universe for tweets that match your terms. If you click on the Advanced Search link to the right of the search button, you can specify even more granular search parameters and filters.

One of my favorites is to search for tweets that are within a certain geographic area (based on user profile data). For example, you might want to search for the terms "need a Web site," but restrict the search to only Twitter users within your geographic area. This will bring back tweets from people within your area that are looking for Web site help.

The reason I wanted to highlight this feature in this chapter is that once you have defined a search that returns the results you want, you can tell Twitter to turn your query into a filter that runs on its servers and creates an RSS feed that you can subscribe to in your favorite RSS reader. This approach means that your query will run and you will automatically get the results showing up in your RSS reader with no additional effort—a very powerful way to monitor certain keywords that appear within the Twitter stream.

Going one step further than just setting up a search that sends results to an RSS reader, you must now cross over into the world of application programming interfaces (APIs) and data feeds. Don't let these terms intimidate you, because in reality, their purpose is easy to understand.

Understanding APIs

An API is simply a language (or syntax) that one piece of software uses to communicate with another piece of software. It defines the types of actions you can ask one piece of software to perform, and it also defines the type of data that can be returned to the calling software program. In effect, this is a sort of two-way conversation via software between the calling program and the program being called. From a high level, that is all you have to know at this point. If you are a software developer, you will want to consult the official Twitter documentation at apiwiki.twitter.com for details on the API itself.

Two Types of Twitter APIs

If you have decided that you need to interact with Twitter as if you were a user, then you will want to use the Twitter REST API. This is a popular option and is used by some of the third-party tools, such as twitterrific and twhirl. This API essentially lets you do the following tasks:

♦ Access the public timeline

♦ Access your friends timeline

♦ Update your status

♦ Create and send new direct messages

♦ Follow other users

♦ Block other users

♦ And virtually every other action you can take via the Twitter Web site is available via the Twitter API

A second API is also available that lets you send search requests to Twitter. The reason these APIs are separate is that the original creator of the search service that Twitter is using was a third-party, mentioned above, called Summize. Twitter is in the process of integrating these two APIs to more closely resemble each other as REST-ful APIs in the near future. The Search API can be used to find tweets containing a certain word, tweets from a specific user, find tweets to a specific user, tweets that reference a specific user, or find tweets containing a certain hashtag (think topic). You can even specify that your results come from a certain geographic region by specifying a radius around a given longitude and latitude. Twitter uses their users profile data to figure out the geo-location based queries.

Understanding Data Feeds

A data feed differs from an API in that it is really a one way transfer of Twitter data to your computer disk, where you can process it later. You are not calling the Twitter API and asking it to take any action on the Twitter servers per se; rather, you are asking Twitter to send you a dump of data.

So, which one to use . . . the Twitter API or the Twitter Data Feed? To answer this question, you should begin by asking yourself anothr simple question: Do I want the data for offline processing (use the Twitter Data Feed), or do I want to interact with Twitter in near real time (use the Twitter API)?

To understand how to automate and leverage the Twitter service, it is important to discuss a few potential ways to do this.

Monitoring

The first level of integration with Twitter is simply to automate the activity of listening to millions of conversations and pulling out the relevant bits of information that are important to you and your business. This information might be competitive intelligence on your toughest competitor, complaints from your own disgruntled customers, or even the identification of market opportunities by monitoring certain keywords.

Imagine that you are in a very competitive market industry where time to market is extremely important. Using Twitter, you could mine the tweets to find out the types of questions your potential clients are asking and then post these to a team blog for further discussion. In fact, we've created a sample application that does just this. Go to www.twitterpower.com/code and you can see how this might work. The sample application allows you to enter in the keywords you want to monitor. As these tweets are captured in a daily dump, the results are posted to a team blog, where your team can discuss the comments of the Twitter users.

Another very valuable aspect of monitoring tweets is to find out what your competition is doing. Imagine being able to see what the Twitter community thinks of your competitor's newest offering. Could that be valuable information? Could you initiate the conversation yourself just to get the tweets going? Here are some valuable insights that I would want to know about my competition:

♦ What are my competitors having trouble with? (could that be a potential opportunity for me?)

♦ What are my competitors getting kudos for? (something I can learn from?)

♦ What do people think of my competition's latest product? (might this be valuable market information?)

But You Aren't Taking Part in "The Conversation"

In terms of the Twitter culture, you have probably heard many times that it is all about "participating in the conversation". From the perspective of an individual, and in a strictly purist sort of way, this is probably true. However, from a business point of view there is much to be gained from simply listening, without the intention of ever participating. This will ruffle the feathers of more than a few who will claim that simply mining tweets for their business intelligence value is a misuse of the original intent of Twitter. Well, it might be, but the data is available and your competition is probably already looking it over. Get over it and get busy.

PARTICIPATING

Taking your automation of Twitter a bit further, we come to the idea of participating. In the context of this chapter, participating means not just listening, but also sending your own tweets in reaction to certain events. From a business perspective, the most obvious example is to send an automated message to those users who decide to follow you. This concept can even be extended beyond the typical "Hey, thanks for following me" message to include a series of messages delivered over the course of a day, week, or longer.

In reality, this mirrors the tools that have been available to marketers for years in the e-mail world in the form of e-mail autoresponders. These are simply tools that let you prewrite a series of messages (in this case, tweets) that can be delivered in response to someone joining your e-mail list (in this case, following you). To show you how easy this is to do, we created a simple Twitter autoresponder for you to try, located at www.twitterpower.com/code.

Another exciting possibility is to join the monitoring capabilities described in the previous section with the autoresponder functionality to create a tool that monitors Twitter for certain keywords, or users, and then autoresponds with valuable comments, content, or links to other relevant resources. Notice I said relevant resources. This kind of tool has the potential to be abused by spammers and people who fill Twitter with unwanted links to sales pages—that is not what I am advocating here.

But imagine a company that monitors tweets to find customers who are expressing dissatisfaction with their product. In response to the tweets they capture, the company automatically sends an invitation to the disgruntled customer to fill out a questionnaire or survey and receive a free coupon for sharing their opinion. In fact, we have set up a simple tool to do just this, and you can access it on our sample code page: www.twitterpower.com/code.

Twitter as a Platform

The final area I would like to explore is using Twitter and its backend services as a universal command line. This has been discussed online in several forums, and I want to expand on the ideas here a bit.

If you think about what is needed to build an application, you really come down to just a few major components. You need a way for users to enter commands; you need something to accept the commands and know what to do with them; you need some storage mechanism that allows you to preserve data over time and between application uses, then retrieve this data later; and finally you need a way to display to the user the results of the command he or she entered. These four major application areas are part of any application (Word, Excel, Photoshop, and even Twitter itself).

What is interesting is that over the past several years, the idea of truly disconnected and distributed applications has not only been accepted, but many of the pieces needed to make this possible are in place. Imagine if we decided to build an application, but only wanted to create the core logic that processed commands. In effect we could build a simple, yet highly useful application that looked like this:

1. User enters commands (via Twitter text box)

2. Accept commands and perform action (we monitor tweets and grab them using the Twitter API, parse them, perform the action via our own service outside Twitter)

3. Store settings and history for later use (we use our own storage)

4. Return results to user (we automate a direct message back to the Twitter user)

By using Twitter as both the input and output mechanism for our sample application, we have eliminated the need to create a user interface. We are simply borrowing the Twitter service as our private user interface. This is an incredibly flexible and interesting way to interact with many backend services. Imagine being able to ask Twitter for a stock quote, a weather report, the status of your flight, etc. Of course, your own code needs to grab the tweets, know how to parse them, perform the requested action, and return the results. We have built a sample program that demonstrates how to do this located at www.twitterpower.com/code. Check out how functional this can be, and tell us about your own solutions.

Summary

We are just beginning to scratch the surface of integrating Twitter and many other social media tools into our core business processes. However, one thing is clear: in today's highly competitive world, integration with valuable resources such as Twitter is an important part of your overall social media strategy.

While Twitter is an incredibly powerful platform that allows you to listen and participate in a universe of conversations, most companies will hire people to sit and interact with Twitter in a manual way. Rather than following that approach, I want to challenge forward-thinking business leaders to consider the benefits of leveraging the power of software to automate much of this interaction in order to find trends, discover hidden opportunities, and outsmart the competition.

12

Play Nice
Legal Considerations

You already know that Twitter is a wonderful way to keep in touch with your friends and business associates. Quick, witty, fun tweets get some great thought-provoking ideas buzzing.

If you are like me, you have probably sent an e-mail you regret (okay, more than once?). The potential to post a tweet that you regret can happen that much faster on Twitter, and it could land you on the bad side of a lawsuit.

While it is true that I have a Harvard shirt I picked up when I visited the campus a few years back, it didn't turn me into a legal expert. (That would sure cut down on tuition fees, wouldn't it?) However, I think it is important to be aware of legal issues surrounding Twitter.

I took some time to consult with Kevin Houchin of Houchin Law in Northern Colorado (houchinlaw.com), and these are some of the considerations he brought to my attention.

I don't want to bore you with a bunch of legalese or scare you away from using Twitter. On the contrary, I want you to practice "Safe Tweet!"

I don't speak legalese, so the following information is direct from the mouth of a bona fide attorney who understands these issues far better than I.

Take it away, Kevin. . . .

I won't be able to cover every possible way you can get yourself in Twitter trouble, but we'll hit the highlights with the most probable ways. Of course each situation is unique to you, your state, the people on the other side, and a bunch of other factors, so don't take my word for it alone. If you find yourself in trouble, consult your own attorney—everybody should own one by now.

Now let's get to it.

The most probable ways you can find yourself in hot water are:

◆ Defamation: damaging someone's reputation

◆ Privacy: disclosing someone else's secrets

◆ Interference with Business Relations

◆ Negligence: harming someone

◆ Contract: ending up in an enforceable agreement

◆ Trademark: confusing consumers about a brand

◆ Copyright: sharing something that's not yours

Defamation

In today's world, we lump harms to someone's reputation arising from a written statement (libel) or from a spoken statement (slander) under the common term "defamation." Here's what we look for:

◆ Defamatory language on the part of the person being accused, which could be you or someone else on Twitter. Note that the language does not have to be direct; it can also be innuendo, satire, etc.

◆ That language must be "of or concerning" the person claiming to be harmed by the language.

◆ The language must be "published," which is assumed in the context of our discussion of a troubling tweet.

◆ The language has to damage the reputation of the person making the complaint. Note that even a statement of opinion might be trouble, for instance: "I don't think Silvia can be trusted with the key to the store" would be actionable because you're implying a personal knowledge and accusation of dishonesty that would harm Silvia's reputation.

If the language refers to a "public figure" or involves a "matter of public concern," then we have to also prove:

♦ Falsity of the language

♦ Fault on the part of the accused person

Remember that you can get in trouble with statements that target an individual, company, association, or anyone that has a reputation to be damaged. And it could cost you big-time, especially if you are referring to a few special cases such as a statement that goes to a business or professional reputation, says someone has a "loathsome disease," has committed a "crime involving moral turpitude," or imputes "unchaste behavior to a woman."

Finally, know this: even a truthful statement can get you into Twitter Trouble if sharing that bit of truth damages someone's reputation. Of course there are all kinds of twists and turns these cases can take, but I'm betting you'll stop reading if I spend any more time belaboring the details.

Privacy

This one is touchy. If you disclose something that a "reasonable person" would not want disclosed, then you could wind up in trouble, even if the disclosures are truthful. An example would be disclosing the real name and location of someone in witness protection.

Another example would be attributing to someone views he doesn't hold, or saying someone did something they did not do. Note that this right is personal, companies can not claim a right of privacy, although they have other avenues to pursue similar situations, such as "Intentional Misrepresentation," otherwise known as "fraud" or "deceit." I could go into those here too, but again, I think you'll stop reading and we have a few more big points to cover.

Interference with a Business Relationship

To get in trouble here, you have to know about a valid contractual relationship, or a valid expectation that someone will be entering a valid relationship, then you have to intentionally mess it up. Of course there are more details to these cases too, but having this in the back of your mind will keep you out of trouble in most situations.

Negligence

Think of a car accident. Now think of a car accident on Twitter, and you'll be heading down the road to understanding this potential problem. In a car accident, you have a duty to conform to a specific standard of conduct, which was breached in the accident and caused actual damage to someone. The same can happen on Twitter. Do you have some duty of care? A good example would be an attorney or doctor, who has a duty to keep client information secret. Did you breach that duty, and did your breach cause damage? All for elements have to be in place to get you in trouble under a negligence theory.

Contract

All it takes to fall into a contract is for there to be an offer made, that offer accepted, and a promise to pay made. That's it. You might think you're joking around on Twitter exchange, but just a single post and response could bind you into some contractual action. Watch out that you don't agree to something you really don't want to do just because you don't think Twitter exchanges count as contractual language. Heck, you could also get in trouble here by making an offer for business services that are seen as an open offer for everyone. The possibilities are endless.

Trademark

Trademark law is all about protecting someone's investment in their brand, personal or business. It's about consumer confusion. The test for trademark infringement is if an appreciable number of consumers would be confused about the source of some goods or services, thinking those goods or services come from, are affiliated with, or endorsed or sponsored by the person making the complaint. The affiliation and endorsement factors will get you in trouble. So don't use someone else's brand name for your Twitter name.

Copyright

I admit, it will be hard to get yourself into a copyright infringement situation based on a single 140-character tweet, but you might be tempted to post a few tweets in a row to share a short poem or song lyrics. Tread carefully.

Is this list exhaustive? probably not. I'm sure there is some form of legal hot water that you could get yourself into that goes beyond my list. But I'm going to assume that you're not a criminal mastermind and that you're not going to use your Twitter account to harass people or solicit young boys or girls to meet you at the mall for a date.

Use your account for good purposes. Use it to make friends and help people. It's a jungle out there, so be careful and play nice.

13

Putting It All Together

A 30-Day Plan for Dominating Twitter

As you have seen, Twitter is both incredibly basic and incredibly powerful. Twitterers are using the service to network and have fun, but corporations, too, have found that microblogging can have a huge impact on the closeness of their communities, on the traffic they pick up at their Web sites, on their relationships with their customers, and on the reach of their brands.

It's simple to use, enjoyable, and effective.

But I want to make it even simpler for you. Whenever you pick up a new tool, there's always a period of playing, a time in which you get a feel for the way the system works and figure out how to make it work best.

That can be a useful period, but it's also a dangerous one.

Because this isn't a time when they get results, commercial users can start to wonder what all the fuss is about. They don't see their traffic increasing, they don't see their sales rising, and they don't see their follower lists growing at a rate that will have enough of an effect on their brand.

So they stop doing it.

That's a huge waste.

The benefits—and the fun—of Twitter aren't at the beginning, when you're building your follower list. They happen once you're up and running, when you have a community of people to chat with and when you can see people clicking through from your Web site to your Twitter timeline and vice versa.

In this chapter, I'm going to try to get you to that stage as quickly as possible by providing you with a 30-Day Plan for Dominating Twitter.

I'm not going to promise that at the end of the 30 days, if you do everything I suggest here, you'll have a thousand followers or anything of the sort. The degree of success that you have depends too much on the subject of your tweets—and, of course, their quality.

Once your timeline has been set up, you'll also need to continue tweeting, replying, and adding new followers every day. The daily goals are in addition to those basic actions.

Clearly, this plan isn't the only way to build a foundation of success on Twitter or the only schedule you should follow. It is, however, one way in which you can get up, running, and delivering results quickly and easily.

Day 1. Sign Up and Settle In

Begin by completing the registration form. Decide whether your first Twitter timeline will promote your personal brand, your Web site, or your company; choose a username that's suitable and easy to remember; and write a short, snappy bio. Using one of the templates in this book should make that easy for you. Remember, you can always change it later.

For a first-time user, Twitter can look like a strange place in which strange people post odd messages about what they're doing while answering questions from complete strangers.

This is what Twitter's all about, so spend a little time today clicking through followers and reading tweets. You should find that you have to tear yourself away.

You can also sign up for TweetBeep today and create alerts for your company name and products. You might well be surprised to find that people are already talking about you.

Day 2. Create Your Background Image

A day for creativity. Your background image is important, so it's worth doing it right. Using a free template will get you moving quickly, but you might want to contact a designer to produce something unique, or play around with designs yourself.

Take a look at the images used by leading Twitterers at Twitterank for ideas.

Day 3. Read Around

We'll soon be building up a bank of tweets for your new followers to read, so spend today preparing with some dedicated reading of your own. This should be fun, but do read critically. Focus on the sorts of topics you'll be tweeting about, pay attention to the sorts of tweets that generate replies, and note who takes part in the discussions.

You'll probably find that while there are plenty of followers willing to read tweets about a certain subject, it will be the same handful that are the most active in the conversations.

But don't start following yet. You first want to have some tweets to show when those Twitterers visit your timeline.

Day 4. Writing Your First Tweets

This is going to be a day of tweeting. Download a Twitter client such as Twhirl or Twitterific so that you don't have to leave the browser open, and every couple of hours or so, post a quick sentence about what you're doing or thinking.

Don't worry about writing something silly—remember, tweets can be deleted too—but focus on making them entertaining, interesting, and fun. Enjoy yourself, but remember from now on, you're going to be tweeting every day!

Day 5. Start Following

And now things can really get moving. By now you're probably itching to start adding followers. Your reading should have alerted you to the main Twitterers in your field, and with a bank of tweets that show you have something to offer in return, you're ready to start following them.

Hit the "follow" button and see which of them follow you in return. By the end of the day, you should find that you've picked up your first followers—and they might well be important ones.

Don't forget to keep tweeting!

Day 6. Add Friends and Acquaintances—and Start Replying

Start expanding your follower list by looking for your friends, acquaintances, and contacts on Twitter. You might not find many, but you should find some. Once you've added them, don't be afraid to send a reply to one of their tweets. While you can direct message them, replying will give you extra content in your timeline and when they reply back, you'll appear in their timeline, exposing your name to their followers—an easy way to gain additional users.

Day 7. Start Catching Big Followers

By now you'll have a few followers. Some will be the main Twitterers on your topic that you'll have identified during your reading. Others will be people you know who you've found on the site.

Spend today making a real effort to add as followers Twitterers with large follower lists. Use Twellow to identify the main movers in different fields, follow them, and reply to their tweets with interesting, valuable information.

Day 8. Add More Followers

The main Twitterers—the people who post regularly and have long follower lists—are like nodes in a network. That makes them good places to start: every time they reply to you, your name spreads out along their network. But you can travel their networks too.

Spend today checking the followers in their lists. Follow them, reply to their tweets and see how many of them follow you in return.

Day 9. Ask a Question

By now, you should have a long enough follower list to start making use of it.

Tap the information that your followers possess.

Ask a question that you'd like answered, and see if you can pick up an answer.

The question itself won't matter too much today—I just want you to see one thing that Twitter can do for you. You'll be amazed at how much your followers know.

Day 10. Answer a Question

So you've discovered how useful Twitter can be. Now it's time to recognize that you have to pay your dues, too, by answering a question.

If one of your followers has asked something you can answer, you'll have an easy opportunity. If they haven't, though, try using the search page to find someone who posed a query. Follow them, then reply with your answer. They might be surprised, but these sorts of random encounters are part of what makes Twitter so exciting.

Day 11. Have Fun!

Twitter might be a valuable marketing tool, but it's also very enjoyable; and enjoying it is a great sign that you're doing it right and will keep doing it too.

Just relax today and have fun. Write tweets that make you laugh and think, reply to tweets you find interesting, and don't think too much about adding to your followers or keeping them entertained.

If you're entertained, they will be too.

Day 12. Look for Your Evangelists

Now for a change of approach. Some of your followers will be far more active in your timeline than others, replying to your tweets and sending you direct messages. They're among the people you want to encourage and keep entertained.

It's possible that there are others out there too, though, people who mention your Web site or discuss your products on Twitter. Use Twitter's search to draw up a list of your main evangelists and potential promoters.

Day 13. Reel In Your Evangelists

Once you've drawn up your list, start putting it to use. Follow your evangelists, and reply to them as usual, but show that you value their opinion by asking them questions about your product, addressing any issues they've raised, and offering them sneak peeks at projects in the works.

These are the people who will be promoting your name for nothing on Twitter, so it pays to keep them happy!

Day 14. Do Some Customer Service

While evangelists can bring plenty of benefits, you might well find that there's no shortage of people on Twitter not entirely happy with your service. Today, you can squash those negative comments.

Search for the name of your product or your company and reply to any complaints with an apology and a request for more information.

Day 15. Post a Link Tweet

You should be tweeting every day, and doing it several times a day, too, so you've probably posted at least one link tweet already, complete with short URL.

Today though, you're going to do it deliberately and measure the results.

Choose a page on your Web site and review the stats for the last week. Post a tweet recommending the page and add a link. The difference in page views might be minimal, but pay attention to the number of ad clicks and the comments left on the page after the tweet. You might well find that your Twitter traffic is small in number but large in influence.

Day 16. Post a Discussion Tweet

And today, we're going to do the same thing with a discussion tweet on Twitter. State an opinion and ask your followers what they think.

Although this won't have any effect on your Web site, it will show you how active your followers are and how willing they are to contribute to your timeline.

Day 17. Post an Action Tweet

A link tweet is one type of action tweet: it encourages your followers to click through to a Web page you recommend. But Twitter can deliver much more powerful results than that.

Today, you can see the results.

Encourage your followers to take an action that will deliver something of value. You could recommend an affiliate product and include a link or ask people to join your mailing list, for example.

Don't expect too much at this stage—it's early days still—but few things are more encouraging than seeing your followers earn you money.

Day 18. Start Putting Your Tweets Together

Over the last few days, you'll have been experimenting with different kinds of tweets. You should have been enjoying the results, too. Today, you can try creating a tweet sequence that leads to an action tweet.

Start by deciding what action you want your followers to take at the end of the sequence. Then, use TweetLater to create a series of tweets, spaced throughout the day that guide your followers to that action.

Day 19. Try a Different Sequence

And today, you can do the same thing but with a different sequence of tweets and a different action at the end. That will let you compare two different tweet sequences to see which delivers the best results.

You'll be spending a lot of time testing tweets and tweet sequences, so this is a good chance to practice!

Day 20. Have Fun!

You've been driving your followers fairly hard during the last two days, so pull back today. Tweet, join discussions, and read other people's timelines while looking for new people to follow.

It will be a break for your followers—and for you, too!

Day 21. Do Some Off-Twitter Marketing

By now, your timeline should be moving along nicely. You should have a reasonable-sized number of active followers (remember, you only need to have more than 10 to be doing better than half of Twitter's users, and more than 80 to be in the top 10 percent!), and you've already felt the benefits of driving those followers to take action.

Today, you can extend your follower list even further by doing some off-Twitter marketing. Register at TwitThis to add their icon to your blog posts. Post a Twitter badge on your Web site, and make sure that your e-mail and forum signatures include your Twitter URL.

And don't forget to keep track of the results so that you can measure the effect.

Day 22. Combine Your Social Media Tools

Some more off-Twitter marketing today, but this time we're going to use the power of your other social media tools.

If you're using Facebook, add the Twitter application to your account so that your tweets turn up on your Facebook page, too. Mention your timeline on your other social media accounts to make sure that people know what you're doing and come to see what you're up to.

And if you're not yet using other social media tools, this is a good time to start!

Day 23. Drive Followers to Purchase a Special Offer

Now we're going to start moving up a level. You've already done the basics and you've seen the results, so let's make things a little more complex. Over the next few days, you're going to be driving your followers to take actions that are more valuable and tougher to carry out than you've done in the past.

Start by driving your followers to purchase something with a special offer. You could use one of your own products with a special discount code, or set up an affiliate relationship with a retailer that lets you offer a cut price.

You can then either create a tweet sequence that primes your followers before dropping in the call to action, or just throw it in and see what happens. Whichever you choose, be sure to record the results.

Day 24. Drive Followers to a Blog

Persuading people to purchase is always going to be a little tricky, so now do something easier: link to your blog.

Don't just put up a Twitterfeed-style headline, though; announce that a new post has gone up and invite people to comment. Find out what happens to your discussions when you really push your followers onto your blog.

Day 25. Drive Followers to Subscribe

Follow up yesterday's Twitter goal by turning those followers into RSS subscribers.

You could try doing that by bringing the discussion on your blog back onto Twitter. Ask your followers what they thought about the post, talk about it during the day, and at the end of the day, urge them to become subscribers.

Day 26. Drive Followers to Purchase Without a Special Offer

Now for the big one. Persuading followers to buy with a special offer is relatively easy. You've made them feel part of an exclusive club and rewarded them for following your tweets. If you are just inviting them to buy, though, you'll have to work a little harder.

Create a series of tweets that discuss the product you want to sell—an affiliate product will do. End with the call to action and track the results. Whether you generate sales or not, you'll have a baseline to which you can compare your future promotions.

Day 27. Have Fun!

And after all that effort, another fun day to show your followers that you value them and not just their wallets.

Day 28. Create a Second Timeline

With your timeline moving along nicely, you're ready to set up a second account. Not everyone needs to do this, but having more than one timeline can be a useful way to create separate brands for different products.

You can even use this second timeline just for automated tweets.

Day 29. Find Followers for Your New Timeline

Spend today building followers for your new timeline. You might not have to work too hard for this, depending on what you want your timeline to do. For an automated timeline powered by Twitterfeed, just telling the followers on your first list about it could be enough.

Day 30. Have Fun!

And finally, end your 30-day crash course the way you mean to go on: by enjoying yourself with tweets, replies, and chats with your growing list of followers.

14

Power Twitterers

In a way, Twitter can be classified as a broadcast channel. And like other channels, Twitter has its own celebrities. While @barackobama has more followers than anyone else, his political campaign used Twitter only for one-way communication. I'm sorry to say that he didn't actually tweet while on the campaign trail.

But there are other Twitter users with tens of thousands of followers who use the site to truly build relationships and interact with other members. They run the gamut from actors and sports figures to CEOs and industry pundits. This chapter spotlights just a few of these "Power Twitterers."

Robert Scoble (@scobleizer)

Self-described "tech-geek blogger," Scoble is a tech enthusiast and video podcast evangelist. His contributions to *Fast Company* magazine spotlight the ways in which new technology is changing the Internet. The majority of Scoble's tweets are replies to his followers. With plenty to say about social media, he can frequently be found tweeting about FriendFeed, Facebook, Google, Qik, and Flickr. Scoble averages 24 tweets/day and is likely to interact if your tweet is engaging and on topic. Follow Robert Scoble at twitter.com/scobleizer or visit his site at Scobleizer.com.

Gary Vaynerchuk (@garyvee)

Entering the Twitter scene in 2007 and becoming a Twitter "rock star" in 2008, Gary Vaynerchuk is a poster child for social media and the way in which the Web is launching people to celebrity status. Simply put, Vaynerchuk is passionate about wine. To be more specific, he believes that the wine-tasting culture has become too exclusive for the average Joe. And that's a shame, because there is no reason everyone of legal age shouldn't be able to enjoy the experience. His Web-based broadcast of WineLibrary.tv reaches "the everyman" with down-to-earth wine analysis and a healthy helping of good-natured fun. With his irreverent approach and valuable insights, Vaynerchuk has caught the attention of the mainstream media with appearances on *Conan, Ellen, Nightline*, and a number of other shows. He averages 10 tweets/day and you can follow him at twitter.com/garyvee or visit his site at WineLibrary.tv.

Peter Shankman (@skydiver)

There's more to publicity than sending a press release, and no one knows this better than Peter Shankman. CEO of The Geek Factory, a boutique marketing and PR strategy firm in New York City, Shankman is notorious for helping clients create events that get media attention. Along with working with some of the biggest corporations in the world, Shankman is frequently invited as a pundit on major national and international news channels. The accomplishment that is getting him more recent attention is his three-times-daily e-mail newsletter, "Help a Reporter Online." This free publication connects journalists with the sources they require. With over 36,000 members as of this writing, Shankman's grassroots endeavor is providing PR opportunities in the unlikeliest of places. He averages six tweets/day; you'll want to watch him for potential media opportunities that may come your way. He is a self-confessed ADHD thrill seeker and you can keep up with Peter's latest stunts at twitter.com/skydiver or visit his site at Shankman.com.

Kevin Rose (@kevinrose)

Digg.com has become one of the world's most popular and influential social bookmarking sites. As founder and site architect of Digg, Kevin Rose has become a social media celebrity who wholeheartedly embraces the spotlight. Along with his flamboyant co-host Alex Albrecht, Rose broadcasts his weekly Web show," *Diggnation*, to scores of loyal viewers. Kevin has tens of thousands of followers on Twitter, yet he does not follow as many in return. Nevertheless, he tweets an average of seven times/day via his iPhone. You'll frequently find him discussing technology and rock climbing. Follow Kevin at twitter.com/kevinrose or visit his site at KevinRose.com.

Guy Kawasaki (@guykawasaki)

A technology evangelist and managing director of an early-stage venture capital firm, Guy Kawasaki is well-known throughout the technology and business sectors. A Stanford and UCLA graduate, Kawasaki is a high-profile public figure known for his time at Apple Computer, Inc., as well as for his numerous books. Extremely active on Twitter, he is known to tweet an average of 30 times/day. Frequently promoting his latest venture, AllTop.com, an online magazine rack of popular topics, Kawasaki tweets a mix of AllTop articles and replies to his followers. You can follow him at twitter.com/guykawasaki or visit his site at GuyKawasaki.com.

Michael Arrington (@techcrunch)

Founder of TechCrunch.com, a weblog dedicated to "obsessively profiling and reviewing new Internet products and companies," Michael Arrington is an active Twitter user known for tweeting tech news. Discussing everything from Microsoft and Google to Mobile and MySpace, Arrington tweets an average of 13 times/day. This is a great follow if you want to keep up with the latest tech news. You can follow Arrington at twitter.com/techcrunch or visit his site at TechCrunch.com.

Wil Wheaton (@wilw)

Best known for starring in the hit film *Stand by* Me and his recurring role as Ensign Wesley Crusher on *Star Trek: The Next Generation*, Wil Wheaton's Twitter bio states, "I'm just this guy, you know?" Not one to follow others at random, Wheaton is a self-professed geek and libertarian who has embraced Twitter as a platform for sharing his views. Tweeting an average of seven times/day, Wheaton's entries are more of a "life-cast" than promotion of any particular projects or reporting of current events. True to Twitter's original intent, he uses the site to state what he is doing right now. You can follow Wheaton at twitter.com/wilw or visit his site at wilwheaton.typepad.com.

MC Hammer (@mchammer)

Massively famous for his baggy pants and smooth dance moves in the 1990s, Hammer's "You Can't Touch This" still reverberates in clubs and parties all over the world. Since signing up for Twitter in the summer of 2008, Hammer has become an avid Tweeter, averaging 10 entries/day. Plugged into politics and culture, he has embraced the spirit of Twitter and regularly shares his thoughts on topics of the day while interacting with fans in a cordial and humble manner—another great example of how celebrity can cultivate an even more engaged and endearing fan base. You can follow Hammer at twitter.com/MCHammer or visit his site at DanceJam.com.

Chris Brogan (@chrisbrogan)

Chris Brogan is a social media advisor who helps businesses and individuals leverage technology to accomplish their goals. A very active Twitter member, Brogan is engaged and interacts with his followers on a regular basis. With an average of 35 tweets/day, he mixes his technology commentary with plenty of real-life dialogue. To expert Twitterers like Chris, it's all part of the same thing. The discussion doesn't begin and end—it just is. You can follow Brogan at twitter.com/chrisbrogan or visit his site at ChrisBrogan.com.

Shaquille O'Neal (@The_Real_Shaq)

Hoops superstar O'NeaHoops superstar O'Neal signed up for Twitter in November 2008 and immediately began tweeting an average of nine times/day. In just 30 days, word spread that this basketball legend had joined the Twitter ranks and nearly 20,000 people became followers. The first to admit that his typing is subpar, O'Neal clearly enjoys sharing his current thoughts and happenings. From commenting on the Phoenix Suns' recent performance to letting us know he has just seen *The Punisher* on DVD, Shaq appears excited to have this new technology in his life. He shoots, he scores! You can follow O'Neal at twitter.com/The_Real_Shaq.

Justine Ezarik (@ijustine)

Hailing from Los Angeles, Justine Ezarik brings her own sense of femininity and Internet savvy to social media. Her videos and tweets are meant to entertain and . . . well, entertain. Self-described Mac user, blogger, and Internet user, the online persona of iJustine is a what-you-see-is-what-you-get experience. Averaging eight tweets/day, Justine is a breath of fresh air in a world that often takes itself way too seriously. You can follow Justine at twitter.com/ijustine or visit her blog at TastyBlogSnack.com.

CONCLUSION

Twitter is surprising. The idea is ridiculously simple. But the benefits—and the enjoyment—are incredible. It's addictive, it's fun, and it's very, very effective.

For Web users, it's a great way to keep in touch. For online publishers, nothing makes readers and customers feel closer. And for commercial users, it's a hugely powerful branding tool.

In this book, I've introduced some of the ways in which Twitter can help with online marketing.

I began by putting Twitter in context. The site is just one—although by far the most successful—of the microblogging services available on the Web, and it's a part of the social media phenomenon that has revolutionized the Internet and the world of publishing.

Understanding that anyone with a computer and a connection to the Internet now has the power to speak to millions of people around the world is vital to recognizing what Twitter and other social media services can do.

The power to broadcast is in your hands—and the power to earn from those broadcasts too.

That's especially true of Twitter, whose users are made up largely of high-earning, highly educated professionals. When you send out tweets to your followers, you can be sure that they're being read by a valuable market, one that can also supply all sorts of useful information and connections, too.

So it's important to start right, with a username that's easy to remember, a bio that explains who you are, and a background image that builds your brand and guides curious new followers to your commercial Web sites. I explained how to do that.

And I talked, too, about building a following on Twitter and how to create a follower list that balances high-quality, key followers with large numbers of readers.

227

Keeping that list growing, though, will depend on producing the right tweets—short posts that are entertaining, informative, and fun, that follow tweet etiquette, and that drive follower behavior.

But persuading followers to take action isn't the only thing you can do with them. Twitter's users are a valuable source of ideas and feedback, and the site can function as a very useful communication tool. I explained how to make the most of both of those methods.

I then talked about how major companies are using Twitter to build a brand, and reviewed some of the most important strategies for communicating your brand's message.

I also talked in detail about using tweet sequences to drive followers to take specific actions, introduced some of the most important tools that extend the use of Twitter, and revealed how to build powerful solutions on top of Twitter's basic platform.

Finally, I provided you with one possible 30-day schedule to get up and running quickly with Twitter.

All of the methods in this book can help anyone to build a long follower list and market their products, their business, or their Web sites with Twitter.

The results can certainly be impressive, but perhaps the most surprising thing about Twitter is just how much fun reading and writing 140-character posts can be. There are few marketing tools that both deliver a powerful punch and are such a blast to use.

So if you decide to use only strategy on Twitter as a result of reading this book, make it this one:

Have fun.

On Twitter, that's a pretty good indication you're doing it right.

Be sure to follow me on Twitter, and I'll look forward to continuing the conversation with you!

twitter.com/joelcomm
www.JoelComm.com

Directory of Twitterers

I've mentioned a lot of Twitterers in this book, and there are plenty of other Twitterers who I think do great work that I didn't mention. Take a look at their timelines and see what you can learn from the way they use Twitter.

Companies

Amazon (twitter.com/amazondeals)

BestBuy (twitter.com/gina_community)

Carnival Cruise Lines (twitter.com/CarnivalCruise)

Cleartrip (twitter.com/cleartrip)

Comcast (twitter.com/comcastcares)

Dell Cloud Computing (twitter.com/dellintheclouds)

Dell Small Business (twitter.com/DellSmallBiz)

Dell Your Blog (twitter.com/dellyourblog)

Delta Airlines (twitter.com/deltaairlines)

Direct2Dell (twitter.com/direct2dell)

GM (twitter.com/GMblogs)

Forrester (twitter.com/forrester)

The Home Depot (twitter.com/thehomedepot)

Jet Blue (twitter.com/JetBlue)

M&Ms (twitter.com/msgreen) (twitter.com/mmsracing)

SmartyPig (twitter.com/smartypig)

SpringLeap (twitter.com/springleap)

Starbucks (twitter.com/starbucks)
(twitter.com/mystarbucksidea)

Whole Foods Market (twitter.com/wholefoods)

Zappos (twitter.com/zappos)

Institutions

The American Red Cross (twitter.com/redcross)

British Parliament (twitter.com/UKParliament)

Individuals

Alaia Williams (twitter.com/cogentdiversion)

Alejandro Reyes (twitter.com/successfool)

Andrew Sims (twitter.com/sims)

Angie Jones (twitter.com/fitbizwoman)

Barack Obama (twitter.com/barackobama)

"Betty Draper" (twitter.com/betty_draper)

Bill Gates (twitter.com/billgates)

Brian Willms (twitter.com/brianwillms)

Carrie Wilkerson (twitter.com/barefoot_exec)

Charles Trippy (twitter.com/CharlesTrippy)

Chris Pirillo (twitter.com/chrispirillo)

Christina Hills (twitter.com/christinahills)

Cyruseftos (twitter.com/cyruseftos)

Dan Nickerson (twitter.com/dannickerson)

Darren Rowse (twitter.com/problogger)

Dave Baldwin (twitter.com/highonbeingdave)

Dave Taylor (twitter.com/DaveTaylor)

David Lawrence (twitter.com/dhlawrencexvii)

Deborah Micek (twitter.com/CoachDeb)

"Don Draper" (twitter.com/don_draper)

Ed Dale (twitter.com/ed_dale)

Gary Vaynerchuk (twitter.com/garyvee)

Hephail (twitter.com/hephail)

James Buck (twitter.com/jamesbuck)

Jason Cormier (twitter.com/jasoncormier)

Jayxtreme (twitter.com/jayxtreme)

Jeremy Schoemaker (twitter.com/shoemoney)

John Reese (twitter.com/johnreese)

Jonathan Fields (twitter.com/jonathanfields)

Lance Armstrong (twitter.com/lancearmstrong)

Mari Smith (twitter.com/MariSmith)

Mashable (twitter.com/mashable)

MC Hammer (twitter.com/MCHammer)

Mike Filsaime (twitter.com/MikeFilsaime)

Natalie Jost (twitter.com/natalie)

Pastor Carlos Whittaker (twitter.com/loswhit)

Perry Belcher (twitter.com/perrybelcher)

Robert Scoble (twitter.com/scobleizer)

Shaquille O'Neal (twitter.com/THE_REAL_SHAQ)

Shel Israel (twitter.com/ShelIsrael)

Stephen Colbert (twitter.com/stephencolbert)

Stephen Fry (twitter.com/stephenfry)

Steve Jobs (twitter.com/stevejobs)

Trudy Valencia (twitter.com/estediava)

Wayne Sutton (twitter.com/waynesutton)

Wil Wheaton (twitter.com/wilw)

Yanik Silver (twitter.com/yaniksilver)

Web Sites

Famous Tweet (www.FamousTweet.com)

Marketing Tweet (www.MarketingTweet.com)

TwitPrw (www.TwitPwr.com)

Other Books by Joel Comm

THE ADSENSE CODE

WWW.THEADSENSECODE.COM

The definitive guide to making money with Google's AdSense programmer for site publishers, this 230-page book provides the strategies and techniques used to generate passive income with any content-based Web site. A *New York Times* bestseller, Comm's easy-to-read and -apply instructions have been applauded by thousands of readers. The hands-on solutions address the concerns and challenges faced by content publishers in their quest to attract targeted traffic, improve content relevance, and increase revenue streams. The world's recognized expert on Google AdSense, Joel Comm provides you with the keys you need to "crack" the AdSense Code and unlock the secrets to making money online. (ISBN 1933596708).

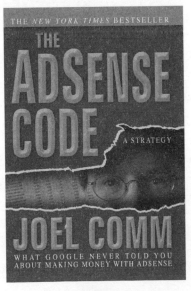

233

CLICK HERE TO ORDER: STORIES OF THE WORLD'S MOST SUCCESSFUL INTERNET MARKETING ENTREPRENEURS

WWW.CLICKHERETOORDERBOOK.COM

Most people associate being an Internet millionaire with the dot-com craze of the late 1990s. But a small band of Internet marketing pioneers were quietly making their fortune before anyone Googled the term "making money online." *Click Here to Order* shows how ordinary people became Internet millionaires by applying their skills, talent, and passion to the Internet. Learn the history of the Internet from the 1960s to the present day, and be inspired by the stories of those who paved the way for the rest of us. Features stories of legendary Internet marketing figures, such as Mark Joyner, Armand Morin, John Reese, Yanik Silver, Jeff Walker, and many more! (ISBN 1600371736).

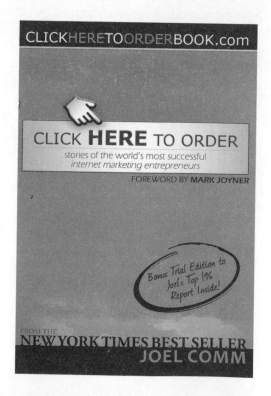

Index

Special Offer!

JOEL COMM'S

ADMIT ONE

FOUR WEEK ONLINE
SOCIAL MEDIA WORKSHOP

"Social Media Sites Have Helped Me Generate Millions In Online Revenue, And Become a NY Times Bestseller.

   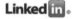   **And Many More..**

Let me share my secrets in my Four Week Online Social Media Workshop. Extensive video instruction and easy to follow guides will show you step-by-step how to leverage all the Major Social Media sites.

- ✓ Increase Your Traffic
- ✓ Improve Your Branding
- ✓ Expand Your Personal and Professional Network

A $197.00 Value – Access Free Today!
http://www.twitterpower.com/workshop

Join the conversation.

Now you know.

wiley.com